1st EDITION

Perspectives on Modern World History

The Women's Liberation Movement

1st EDITION

Perspectives on Modern World History

The Women's Liberation Movement

Sylvia Engdahl

Editor

GREENHAVEN PRESS
A part of Gale, Cengage Learning

GALE
CENGAGE Learning·

Detroit • New York • San Francisco • New Haven, Conn • Waterville, Maine • London

GALE
CENGAGE Learning

Elizabeth Des Chenes, *Managing Editor*

© 2012 Greenhaven Press, a part of Gale, Cengage Learning.

Gale and Greenhaven Press are registered trademarks used herein under license.

For more information, contact:
Greenhaven Press
27500 Drake Rd.
Farmington Hills, MI 48331-3535
Or you can visit our Internet site at gale.cengage.com.

For product information and technology assistance, contact us at
Gale Customer Support, 1-800-877-4253.

For permission to use material from this text or product, submit all requests online at
www.cengage.com/permissions.

Further permissions questions can be e-mailed to permissionrequest@cengage.com.

Articles in Greenhaven Press anthologies are often edited for length to meet page requirements. In addition, original titles of these works are changed to clearly present the main thesis and to explicitly indicate the author's opinion. Every effort is made to ensure that Greenhaven Press accurately reflects the original intent of the authors. Every effort has been made to trace the owners of copyrighted material.

Cover image © Bettmann/Corbis.

LIBRARY OF CONGRESS CATALOGING-IN-PUBLICATION DATA
The women's liberation movement / Sylvia Engdahl, book editor.
     p. cm. -- (Perspectives on modern world history)
  Includes bibliographical references and index.
  ISBN 978-0-7377-5790-3 (hardcover)
  1. Feminism--United States. 2. Women's rights--United States. I. Engdahl, Sylvia.
  HQ1421.W6597 2012
  305.420973--dc23
                                                                                   2011039803

Printed in the United States of America
 2 3 4 5 6 7 16 15 14 13 12

CONTENTS

not accept women, and married women could not get credit in their own names.

CHAPTER 2   Controversies Surrounding the Women's
Liberation Movement

they are less productive, and that the preference of many for domestic roles is their free
choice, not the result of alleged brainwashing
or oppression by men.

A magazine supportive of women's liberation answers questions commonly raised by
women who do not feel that the movement
is needed. It argues that it is important to
change social custom and give up the idea
that women are dependent on men, and that
liberated women do not neglect their children,
as is sometimes claimed, but are able to give
more to them.

A member of the US Congress, who later
became the first woman to seek nomination
for the presidency, argues in the House of
Representatives in favor of the ERA, saying
that she has experienced more discrimination
because she is a woman than because she is
black and that it is wrong for prejudice against
women to be considered acceptable.

In testimony before a US Senate committee on
the ERA, a prominent activist argues that the
injustices suffered by women stem from the
mistaken beliefs that women are biologically

inferior to men, that they are already treated equally in American society, that children need full-time mothers, and that the women's liberation movement will not last.

ratified. However, she says, changing laws will not be enough; there must be a change in the way women are viewed in everyday life, and the work of those who choose homemaking must be valued.

rights treaties were not sufficient to protect women's rights, developed a treaty called the Convention on the Elimination of All Forms of Discrimination against Women. It was adopted by the General Assembly in 1979 and went into force upon ratification in 1981.

Susan Faludi

In the 1980s, some women began to feel that despite all that had been gained from women's liberation, it had made them more unhappy than before. The media paid a great deal of attention to this backlash. Supporters of the movement, however, maintained that though equality with men had by no means been achieved, the majority of women believed their lives had been improved.

CHAPTER 3

Personal Narratives

Phyllis LaFata, interviewed by Ann B. Lever

In a 1972 interview, a founding member of the St. Louis chapter of the National Organization for Women describes how she became involved in the women's liberation movement and the goals she feels are important.

Joan

In a 1971 article, a woman who was initially against the women's liberation movement while in college explains why she changed her mind. She realized that she should not have to fake feminine charm to please society nor need a strong man to look up to.

FOREWORD

"History cannot give us a program for the future, but it can give us a fuller understanding of ourselves, and of our common humanity, so that we can better face the future."

—Robert Penn Warren,
American poet and novelist

The history of each nation is punctuated by momentous events that represent turning points for that nation, with an impact felt far beyond its borders. These events—displaying the full range of human capabilities, from violence, greed, and ignorance to heroism, courage, and strength—are nearly always complicated and multifaceted. Any student of history faces the challenge of grasping the many strands that constitute such world-changing events as wars, social movements, and environmental disasters. But understanding these significant historic events can be enhanced by exposure to a variety of perspectives, whether of people involved intimately or of ones observing from a distance of miles or years. Understanding can also be increased by learning about the controversies surrounding such events and exploring hot-button issues from multiple angles. Finally, true understanding of important historic events involves knowledge of the events' human impact—of the ways such events affected people in their everyday lives—all over the world.

Perspectives on Modern World History examines global historic events from the twentieth-century onward by presenting analysis and observation from numerous vantage points. Each volume offers high school, early college level, and general interest readers a thematically arranged anthology of previously published materials that address a major historical event, with an emphasis on international coverage. Each volume opens with background information on the event, then presents the controversies surrounding that event, and concludes with first-person narratives from people who lived through the event or were affected by it. By providing primary sources from the time of the event, as well as relevant commentary surrounding the event, this series can be used to inform debate, help develop critical thinking skills, increase global awareness, and enhance an understanding of international perspectives on history.

Material in each volume is selected from a diverse range of sources, including journals, magazines, newspapers, nonfiction books, personal narratives, speeches, congressional testimony, government documents, pamphlets, organization newsletters, and position papers. Articles taken from these sources are carefully edited and introduced to provide context and background. Each volume of Perspectives on Modern World History includes an array of views on events of global significance. Much of the material comes from international sources and from US sources that provide extensive international coverage.

Each volume in the Perspectives on Modern World History series also includes:

- A full-color **world map**, offering context and geographic perspective.
- An annotated **table of contents** that provides a brief summary of each essay in the volume.
- An **introduction** specific to the volume topic.
- For each viewpoint, a brief **introduction** that has notes about the author and source of the viewpoint, and that provides a summary of its main points.
- Full-color **charts**, **graphs**, **maps**, and other visual representations.

- Informational **sidebars** that explore the lives of key individuals, give background on historical events, or explain scientific or technical concepts.
- A **glossary** that defines key terms, as needed.
- A **chronology** of important dates preceding, during, and immediately following the event.
- A **bibliography** of additional books, periodicals, and websites for further research.
- A comprehensive **subject index** that offers access to people, places, and events cited in the text.

Perspectives on Modern World History is designed for a broad spectrum of readers who want to learn more about not only history but also current events, political science, government, international relations, and sociology—students doing research for class assignments or debates, teachers and faculty seeking to supplement course materials, and others wanting to improve their understanding of history. Each volume of Perspectives on Modern World History is designed to illuminate a complicated event, to spark debate, and to show the human perspective behind the world's most significant happenings of recent decades.

INTRODUCTION

The twentieth century was a time of change: technological change, with the advent of automobiles, airliners, and computers; political change, brought about by two world wars and a number of lesser ones; and social change, most notably the winning of civil rights for African Americans. But perhaps no change had greater impact on the average American's life than the alteration of the role of women.

At the beginning of the century, it was taken for granted that men and women differed in more than their bodily characteristics. Women were assumed to have different capabilities, mental as well as physical, which were considered by most people to be inferior to those of men. There were exceptions, of course; there have been outstanding women throughout history, probably far more than history records. But they were viewed as rarities and irrelevant to what was expected of women in general. Equality between the sexes was a concept most people would have laughed at. Women, it was thought, were intended by nature to be mothers and homemakers with no interest in business, professional careers, or public affairs. They were not even allowed to vote.

After the upheavals produced by World War I, some women began to question these assumptions. Traditional restrictions on female dress and behavior were crumbling; short skirts and bobbed hair became acceptable, long black stockings were no longer required with swimsuits, and dating customs became more relaxed. In 1920, due to the efforts of the activists known as suffragists, women gained the right to vote in the United States through the Nineteenth Amendment to the Constitution. But in other respects their status did not change.

Few careers were open to them; full-time devotion to marriage and motherhood was still considered a girl's natural destiny, unless she failed to attract a man and suffered the unfortunate fate of becoming an old maid.

Homemaking was indeed a full-time job in the early part of the century. Cooking, cleaning, washing and ironing clothes, sewing, and shopping—not to mention caring for children—took all of a woman's time before technology dramatically reduced the hours required. Women who felt a need for other work were mainly those who had servants, which were then affordable for middle-class families. The development of the appliances taken for granted today changed all that. By the time of World War II, most homes had gas or electric stoves, refrigerators, vacuum cleaners, and washing machines (dryers and dishwashers were not common until later). Some women became restless; moreover, they began to lose the sense of accomplishment and importance to society they had previously possessed.

During the war, women were employed in defense plants—factories that produced airplanes, jeeps, and so forth—and in other jobs previously held by men who had joined the armed forces. Many discovered for the first time what it was like to work outside their homes and found that they liked it. Then, after the war when the men came home, most married women with jobs lost them to veterans. At first, few complained; they were happy to have their husbands back and after the uncertainty of war, they welcomed a focus on family. This was the era of the baby boom. By the sixties, however, the babies were teens who needed little care and there were more labor-saving appliances in homes than ever. Underneath, if not consciously, some women began to question the fairness of wives doing all the housework when men were just as capable of operating those devices as they were. Homemaking no longer required special skills, and younger women did not place the value on it that former generations had. They wanted different work, yet the only choice generally available was between unskilled labor or traditionally "female" occupations such as teachers, nurses, and secretaries. This seemed unjust, as did the fact that women who worked were usually paid less than men for the same job.

The restrictions were not absolute. A small minority of women became doctors, scientists, and other professionals, and though outright discrimination against women was common, there were some who never encountered any. Much is made of the fact that want ads in newspapers were segregated by sex, but women who applied for jobs listed under "men" were sometimes hired. On the whole, however, women were held back. When Sandra Day O'Connor, who later became the first female justice of the US Supreme Court, graduated from law school, no legal firm would employ her as a lawyer; she was offered only a secretarial position. Her experience was all too typical.

The time was ripe for protest. When *The Feminine Mystique* by Betty Friedan was published in 1963, there was an overwhelming response from women. That book, which pointed out the prevalent discrimination against women and strongly criticized the system under which girls were taught that to be "feminine" in the eyes of men should be their ambition, is generally considered the inspiration for second-wave feminism (first-wave feminism was the effort to win women's voting rights). It argued that women were the equals of men and could find fulfillment only through work that used their full mental capacity.

In the late sixties the women's liberation movement took form. The National Organization for Women (NOW) quickly grew from a small group aiming to influence legislation on women's rights to the organizer of a nationwide "strike" and march of low-paid women and housewives. The event drew wide media coverage, enlisting many more women among the ranks of protesters. At the same time, more-radical feminists attracted national attention with inflammatory words and demonstrations patterned after those of the civil rights and antiwar movements in which they had previously been active. They were ridiculed by the press and disparagingly called "women's libbers" as a result. But the idea of gender equality gained ground.

Radical feminists wanted more than political, professional, and educational equality; they advocated fundamental changes in American society. Some were lesbians, in an era when acceptance of homosexuality had little or no public support. Many belonged to political groups that opposed capitalism, and even those who did not were passionately devoted both to civil rights for blacks and to the condemnation of the Vietnam War. The concepts of "oppression" by men and "liberation" from the alleged tyranny were derived from this ideological background. The Redstockings, one of the most prominent radical groups, declared: "Women are an oppressed class. . . . In reality, every such relationship [between a man and a woman] is a *class* relationship. . . . All other forms of exploitation and oppression (racism, capitalism, imperialism, etc.) are extensions of male supremacy." Most women did not consider themselves oppressed. Liberation, to them, meant freedom not from men but from the restrictions imposed on them by tradition and from second-class professional status. Radical feminists were a vocal minority unsupported by mainstream groups, and they in turn scorned those groups for not making stronger demands. Nevertheless, the two branches of the movement shared the conviction that rights for women must be guaranteed by law.

The immediate goal of women's liberation advocates was to amend the US Constitution to provide such a guarantee. The Equal Rights Amendment (ERA) was not a new idea; it had in fact been developed shortly after women won the right to vote and had been reintroduced in every Congress since 1923. Few had taken it seriously, however. As the liberation movement took hold, support grew, and in 1972 the ERA was adopted by Congress and submitted to the states to be ratified. Twenty-two states ratified it that year, another eight did so in 1973, and a handful thereafter. It seemed a foregone conclusion that the ERA would soon be part of the Constitution. But thirty-eight states were needed for ratification, five states rescinded their ratifications, and three states short of the total needed, the Amendment stalled.

Public approval of the ERA declined in the mid-seventies largely because of a countermovement. The Stop ERA campaign was launched by conservative women when they realized to their dismay that it was about to become law. Two types of conservatives joined to defeat the amendment. Social conservatives believed—in many cases on a religious basis—that the majority of women found fulfillment in homemaking and motherhood and that this was indeed their natural role. They perceived that if gender equality were legally established, women would lose the special protections in existing laws and the financial support these laws provided to widowed or divorced women. Moreover, many were angered by the liberation movement's downgrading of homemaking. Libertarian conservatives, on the other hand, objected to intervention of the federal government in what they considered private affairs. They did not want to give any more power to the government.

Other feared outcomes of the ERA were the drafting of women for military service and the possibility that servicewomen would be sent into combat; the funding of abortions by taxpayers; the legalization of same-sex marriage; and the alleged likelihood of unisex restrooms. Legal scholars say most of these things would not have been required—and some of them became a reality even without the ERA. These fears were powerful deterrents to its acceptance by the people of the 1970s, and on June 30, 1982, the time legally allowed for ratification expired.

Despite the failure of the ERA, the effort of the grass-roots movement that led to its passage had significant effects on society. Many state and federal women's rights laws were passed, and there were a number of US Supreme Court decisions requiring men and women to be treated as equals. Furthermore, social attitudes toward women shifted. Today, women are employed in all fields and few would question the appropriateness of a girl's career choice. Even the English language has changed, with terms ending in "man" such as "fireman" and masculine pronouns in reference to both sexes having been discarded in favor of gender-neutral wording. Women are now served at all public establishments on the same basis as men. Many people have come to believe that an amendment to the Constitution is no longer necessary because of these changes and because the government already gives women full rights.

Nevertheless, third-wave feminists—women who have been active in denouncing discrimination since the battle for the ERA—believe that an equal rights amendment is needed for its symbolic value. Furthermore, they feel it is wrong that women's average income is less than the average man's. Income inequality between the sexes may be due to women choosing relatively lower paid work or taking time off from paid work to raise families. Whether such women's choices are due to lack of opportunity or to true personal preference is a controversial question, but there is no doubt that today girls have different expectations for their lives than they did only half a century ago.

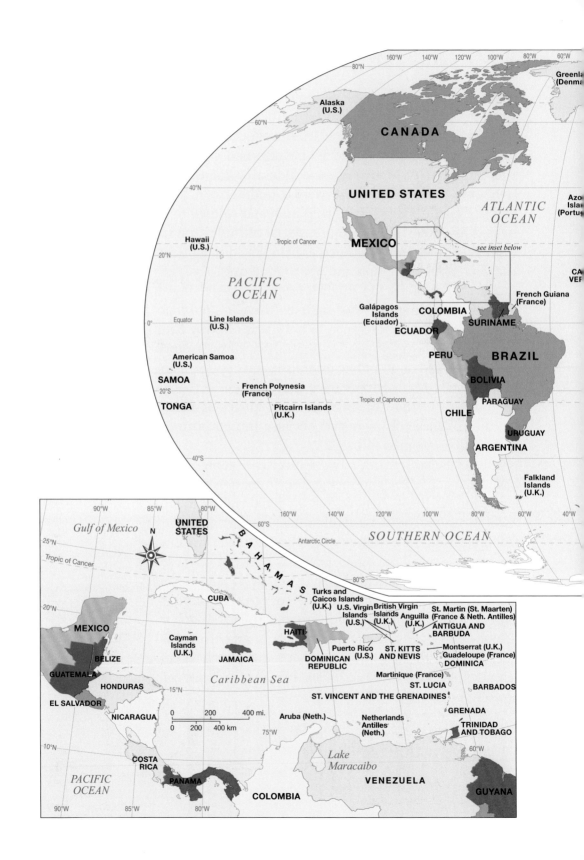

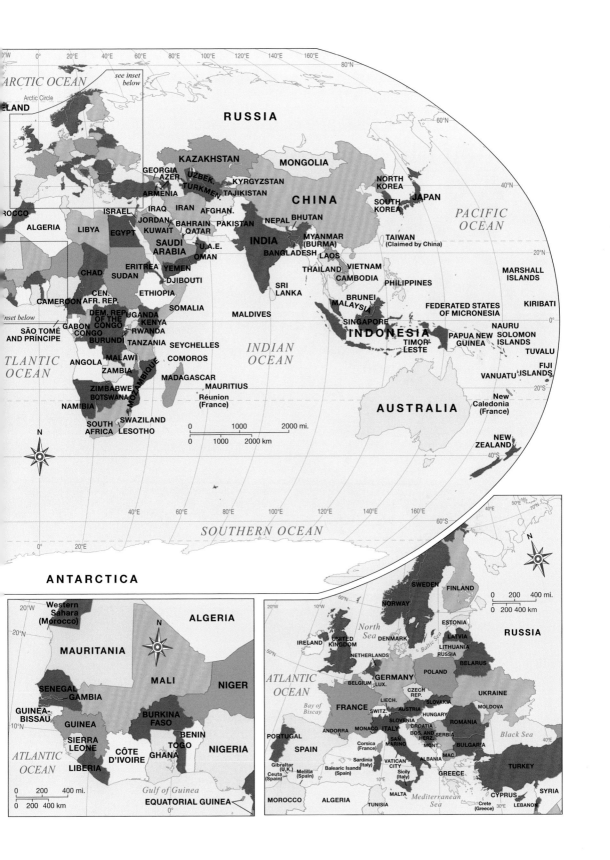

CHAPTER 1

Historical Background on the Women's Liberation Movement

An Overview of the Women's Liberation Movement

Vincent Tompkins

The women's liberation movement was the most significant social movement of the 1970s. It resulted in the passage of laws that reduced discrimination against women in the workplace, and many new careers were opened to women. The US Congress finally adopted an amendment to the Constitution, the Equal Rights Amendment (ERA), proposed many years before, which would have banned all discrimination on the basis of sex. However, due to a grassroots campaign to stop it by conservative women, the amendment was not ratified by enough states to become law. Nevertheless, the movement transformed traditional ideas about the role of women in society, despite divisions among feminists and problems caused by its failure to take into account the needs of low-income women whose marriages ended in divorce.

Photo on previous page: Women attend a Boston rally in support of the Equal Rights Amendment in June 1981. **(Michael Grecco/ Getty Images.)**

One of the most popular advertising campaigns of the early 1970s was that of Virginia Slims cigarettes. The cigarette was thinner than most, but beyond that, hardly remarkable. The ad campaign, however, was an eye grabber. Magazines and bill-boards displayed slender, apparently self-assertive models in the latest fashions clutching the cigarette. The ad copy said, "You've Come a Long Way, Baby." Sometimes featuring an insert photograph of women in turn-of-the-century dress being punished for smoking by police, ministers, or other authority figures, the ad successfully tied cigarette smoking to the burgeoning women's liberation movement. Emphasizing the fact that at one time it was thought unladylike to smoke, the ad implied that to continue smoking Virginia Slims was an act of rebellion against women's traditional roles. Hugely successful as an ad campaign, the caption "You've Come a Long Way, Baby" also embodied for many the triumph of the women's movement and feminism in the 1970s.

> "Women's liberation was to the 1970s what the civil rights movement was to the early 1960s—the most significant social movement in the United States.

New Roles

The women's liberation movement shattered many established traditions of female subordination in American life and opened up a host of heretofore closed occupations to women. Feminism revolutionized women's and men's sense of their gender roles and transformed literary theory, art, and social analysis. Women's liberation was to the 1970s what the civil rights movement was to the early 1960s—the most significant social movement in the United States. Like the civil rights movement, feminism was controversial and never wanted for opponents; like the civil rights movement, the political and social effects of feminism were widespread and deep reaching.

Because the women's movement was so powerful, not only did it rectify a host of injustices in American life, but it also raised important questions which remain unresolved. The Virginia Slims ad campaign, for example, demonstrated the difficulty feminism faced transforming deeply held gender assumptions. As perhaps the most visible everyday reminder of the women's movement, some feminists applauded the ad campaign as reinforcing their conviction that a liberated woman need follow no established social rule save that set by her own conscience. Many feminists, however, were troubled that the antiestablishment women's movement could be so easily appropriated for crassly commercial ends. Many more feminists were troubled that the women in the ad copy were uniformly beautiful and young, unlike the majority of women feminists were attempting to liberate. The ad campaign seemed to many to be the sexist expression of an antisexist philosophy. Such problematic advances, however, were typical of the women's movement in the 1970s. Women had come a long way; they had a long way yet to go.

> "One of feminism's most significant demands was for equal pay for equal work."

Equal Pay

By the 1970s women's liberationists were active on a variety of fronts. Reform of divorce and rape laws, improvement of the health-care system, and promotion of day care were important goals. One of feminism's most significant demands was for equal pay for equal work. Increasing numbers of young women, rejecting the role of suburban housewife, were entering the factory and office. Their mothers followed them into the workplace, pressured by the economic downturn of the decade, which forced many families to seek both male and female sources of income. Neither the young activists nor their

mothers were paid as well as men, on average earning 57 percent of male wages. Women were further short-changed by labor laws passed at the turn of the century that prevented women from working overtime; moreover, like African-Americans, women usually were forced to work the lowest-paid, most menial jobs. Women activists sought to change the conditions in the workplace by appealing to the equal-protection clause of the Fourteenth Amendment. A female lawyer for the American Civil Liberties Union (ACLU), Ruth Bader Ginsburg, hoped to repeat the success the civil rights movement had in challenging inequality in the courts. She won two workplace cases before the Supreme Court, *Reed v. Reed* (1971), and *Frontiero v. Richardson* (1973), both of which confirmed that it was illegal to deny women economic equality with men. The federal government reinforced these claims of job equality. Title VII of the Civil Rights Act of 1964 made job discrimination against women illegal, but the federal agency set up to enforce this law, the Equal Employment Opportunity Commission (EEOC), failed to act on behalf of women for most of the 1960s. In 1970, under a new set of administrators, the EEOC filed suit against American Telephone and Telegraph (AT&T), and won the company's agreement to set up an affirmative-action program. By 1973 the EEOC had filed 147 more suits, and occupational barriers against women began to fall. AT&T hired women to climb up telephone poles and string wire and employed men to sit at desks and operate telephones. The military academies began to admit women, and the Ivy League universities went coed. Even Las Vegas hired female blackjack dealers. By 1974 only Nevada retained laws limiting overtime work for women. Congress passed a host of legislation reinforcing the prohibition on sex discrimination; women even succeeded in gaining a tax deduction for child care in families with both parents working (a similar proposal to establish a national system of day care was vetoed

Photo on previous pages: It was common for women to work in typing pools, like the one in this office in 1959. In 1974 secretaries and typists had the largest proportion of women workers. (**Bert Hardy Advertising Archive/Getty Images.**)

by President Richard Nixon). Much of the progress, however, was more apparent than real. In 1979 women's wages remained an average of 57 percent of men's, and many professional women complained that high-paying, high-prestige jobs were still denied them. To feminists it was clear that the laws on the books were not sufficient. Many sought a new law, in the form of an equal rights amendment to the Constitution.

The ERA

The Equal Rights Amendment (ERA) had first been proposed to Congress in 1923. Resubmitted in a new form, prohibiting discrimination on account of gender, it overwhelmingly passed Congress in March 1973 and was quickly ratified by thirty states. Thereafter the ratification process stalled, several states short of the required three-fourths majority. Part of the problem with passage was that many laws already passed at the state and federal level prohibited discrimination, and the ERA seemed superfluous. The major objection to the ERA, however, was that the amendment was so vague and open-ended as to lead to sweeping changes in American social life. Middle- and working-class women particularly feared the ERA would lead to a loss of alimony in divorce cases, the drafting of women into the military, and the creation of unisex bathrooms. These fears were seized upon and amplified by a female conservative, Phyllis Schlafly, who organized the National Committee to Stop ERA in 1972. Schlafly, a longtime activist in the right wing of the Republican Party, was fundamentally opposed to the ERA on ideological grounds. A militant anti-Communist and opponent of big government, Schlafly feared the ERA would give the government the power to intervene radically in American family life and restructure established

> Animosity toward feminists and their social agenda was a staple of the 1970s.

PROPORTION OF JOBS HELD BY WOMEN IN 1974

	Number of Women Workers	Proportion of Jobs Held by Women
Secretaries	2,922,000	99%
Receptionists	423,000	97%
Typists	980,000	96%
Child-care workers	341,000	96%
Nurses, dieticians	879,000	96%
Hairdressers, cosmetologists	354,000	91%
Bank tellers	252,000	88%
Bookkeepers	1,393,000	88%
Cashiers	864,000	87%
Health-service workers	1,310,000	87%
File clerks	231,000	85%
Librarians	125,000	83%
Counter clerks (nonfood)	243,000	74%
Office-machine operators	480,000	71%
School-teachers	1,988,000	70%
Health technicians	220,000	70%
Food-service workers	2,277,000	70%

Taken from: Vincent Tompkins, ed., "Women's Liberation," *American Decades, Vol. 8, 1970–1979.* Gale, 2001. Original data source: US Department of Labor.

customs and laws regarding marriage, divorce, child custody, and adoption. Schlafly pointed out that because the ERA affected only state and federal governments, it would not change discrimination by private employers. She also suggested to state legislators that the amendment would transfer state power to the federal government. Such arguments were persuasive, but Stop ERA's real power lay in grass-roots organization and in enlisting the fears of many Americans that the pace of social change was proceeding too quickly. Schlafly's organization included local groups such as WWWW (Women Who Want to be Women) and HOW (Happiness of Womanhood), who flooded state capitols with telegrams, phone calls, and homemade breads and pies, and who protested at rallies behind placards reading "Preserve us from a congressional jam; Vote against the ERA sham." Such efforts resulted in several states rescinding their approval of the ERA. In 1979 the ratification period expired. Congress passed a three-year extension, but not a single new state approved the amendment. By 1982 the ERA was dead.

The Abortion Issue

The ERA defeat was symptomatic of a growing conservatism among Americans, both men and women. Sown by economic frustration and harvested by conservative politicians, animosity toward feminists and their social agenda was a staple of the 1970s. Hostility toward women's reproductive rights was particularly pronounced. In the landmark 1973 *Roe v. Wade* case, the Supreme Court decided that women, as part of their constitutional right to privacy, may choose to abort a pregnancy in the first trimester. The decision invalidated many state laws that punished abortion—even as a result of rape, incest, or (rarely) because of the threat to the mother's life—as a criminal offense. . . .

Many feminists supported *Roe* and access to abortion because they felt it was central to a new role for women in American society. Few feminists argued that abortion was a positive good, but they insisted that women had the intellectual capacity—and emotional compassion—to determine for themselves whether or not to terminate a pregnancy. They called their position pro-choice, and in *Roe* the Supreme Court substantially agreed with their outlook. The Supreme Court, however, was ahead of many Americans. Although the majority of respondents in public-opinion polls favored a reform of the strictest abortion laws (but not all of them), many Americans uncomfortable with the changing role of women in American society seized upon the abortion issue as a means of expressing their

PROPORTION OF JOBS HELD BY WOMEN IN 1974 (CONTINUED)		
	Number of Women Workers	Proportion of Jobs Held by Women
Retail clerks	1,600,000	69%
Social workers	195,000	55%
Office managers	132,000	42%
Real-estate agents	128,000	37%
Cleaning-service workers	680,000	33%
Restaurant workers	160,000	32%
Writers, artists, entertainers	284,000	32%
College teachers	130,000	28%
Accountants	155,000	22%
Bank, financial officers	81,000	19%
Sales managers	90,000	16%
Physicians and dentists	58,000	9%
Science technicians	75,000	9%
Policemen, firemen	65,000	5–6%
Lawyers	12,000	4%
Engineers	9,000	Less than 1%
Construction craftsmen	20,000	Less than 1%

Taken from: Vincent Tompkins, ed., "Women's Liberation," *American Decades, Vol. 8, 1970–1979.* Gale, 2001. Original data source: US Department of Labor.

discontent. Often they tied their opposition to abortion to wider protests against the changing character of the times. Prolife for such people often meant more than the defense of the unborn. It meant an attempt to affirm "natural" limits and boundaries—to the family, the community, and the state. Fundamentalist opponents of abortion routinely condemned not only the abortion procedure, but feminists, liberals, relativism, secular humanism, and any philosophy advanced without reference to absolutes. Conservative politicians and televangelists quickly realized the centrality of the abortion issue in the minds of these Americans and used opposition to abortion to construct a tremendous political coalition, one which would seize Congress in 1978 and the presidency in 1980. Ironically, abortion came to hold as central a place in the social philosophy of conservatives as it did in the political theory of feminists.

> The 1970s were a decade filled with female firsts and women's achievements.

Although conservatives mounted the kind of grassroots campaign against abortion they used against the ERA, they had less success. The Hyde Amendment, passed by Congress in 1976, outlawed the use of Medicaid funding to provide abortions; beyond this, however, conservatives proved ineffectual—especially in their general opposition to feminism.

Feminist Achievements

It fact, the 1970s were a decade filled with female firsts and women's achievements. In 1972 women increased their representation in state legislatures by an unprecedented 28 percent. Although Shirley Chisholm, an African-American woman, unsuccessfully challenged male candidates for the Democratic nomination for president that year, Americans sent record numbers of women to Congress. . . . President Nixon appointed the first two women generals in May 1970, and the FBI hired its first female agent in 1972. Women also flooded into the professions. The proportion of women entering law schools increased 500 percent; 40 percent of those entering classes in medical schools were women; and 25 percent of doctorates earned went to women. Women became increasingly visible in the media, especially as journalists. . . .

The real impact of feminism took place at the local level, reshaping the intimate conduct of American life. Like its conservative opposition, women's liberation was also a grassroots movement, and in localities across the nation women established badly needed women's health clinics, rape-crisis centers, and battered-women's shelters. Colleges and universities created women's studies programs. In small communities throughout the United States, women demanded new respect from men, access to better-paying jobs, and an end to sexism in everyday life. More secure with their sexuality and less likely to be pressured into compulsory childbirth, women experimented with premarital and casual sex. Women across the country demanded that men set aside their male chauvinism and belief in male superiority. Women increasingly voiced criticisms of sexism in language and manners. They demanded male help with housework and child care. Feminism also promised to reshape public attitudes toward masculinity as well as to liberate femininity. . . .

Recognizing that as many as 70 percent of the mothers of school-age children work outside the home, the women's movement was vocal in its demands for universal child-care services. By the 1970s most child-welfare specialists and educators joined in lobbying for greater access to these important social services for all children. Congress responded by increased funding for Head Start and other educational programs.

An Intellectual Revolution

Women's liberation inspired the emergence of a sophisticated feminist social theory that promised to further the restructuring of gender roles in the United States. Inverting the radical political theory of the 1960s, feminist intellectuals and academics argued that systematic male domination, which they termed patriarchy, was responsible for many social ills. Patriarchy was manifest not only in sexism but in irresponsible individualism, sterile science, dehumanizing technology, and punitive capitalism—all of which were the result of masculine rationality. Feminists sought to make the world a more empathic, intuitive, and compassionate place. Borrowing an axiom from the New Left, feminists maintained that "the personal is political." A revolution in gender roles and personal relationships would accordingly result in a revolution in the productive apparatus of modern society. More radically, some feminists suggested that patriarchy operated best by hiding its domination in the guise of a "natural" world order. They maintained that traditionally accepted social arrangements—the family, childrearing by women, heterosexuality—were masks for male domination. Such feminists argued that gender was constructed by a set of social and historical relations that privileged men. . . .

The incompatibility of such theoretical formulations with the established order of society led to divisions and political fragmentation among feminists. Younger, more militant feminists such as Robin Morgan sought a full-scale overthrow of society; older feminists, such as Betty Friedan, were more interested in achievable social reform. . . .

Radical lesbians such as Andrea Dworkin argued that, given contemporary social and sexual values, heterosexual intercourse was rape and campaigned against pornography, erotica, and offensive speech which they felt were part of a culture of violence against women.

Such arguments, especially as they became more fixed in the 1980s, mirrored those of male critics of the women's liberation movement who believed that biology is destiny.

Feminism and the Working Class

Conservatives sometimes used such lesbian arguments to discredit feminism among more moderate women and men, but the women's liberation movement as a whole divided naturally—and sharply—over the issue of class. Many older American women hardly felt oppressed by their marriages. For them domesticity was a positive good, and they feared that feminism would corrode the bond of family. Furthermore, many feminist leaders came from privileged backgrounds and limited their critique of society to its limits on opportunities for women of their class. For working-class Americans feminism did not promise access to the boardroom, the university chair, or the legislature, but to dreary factory or clerical work at low wages. Against such a prospect domestic life seemed indeed blissful. Schlafly, sensitive to such fears, was often able to mobilize female support more effectively than left-leaning feminists. Her success forced many feminists to reexamine the implicit elitism of their approach. By the end of the decade, moreover, the concrete results of women's liberation forced many feminists to reconsider their movement soberly. . . .

> Class divisions among feminists were most obvious when considering two issues—child care and divorce.

The class divisions among feminists were most obvious when considering two issues—child care and divorce. Upper-class feminists discussed child care but rarely marshaled their forces to push for increased day care facilities nationally. Wealthy Americans had the economic resources to provide for child supervision in

a two-income family, and feminists pursuing professional careers often were unconcerned with child-care
issues. After President Nixon vetoed day-care legislation
in 1972, women's liberation at the national level abandoned the issue, although ad hoc efforts at the local level
continued to be pursued. The need for quality day care,
medical assistance, and maternity leave became acute as
working-class male income declined and women were
forced to take jobs (usually low-skill, low-paying) outside
the home. By 1976 one-half of all American mothers
were employed. Without a systematic nationwide system
of maternity leave and child care, women often found
themselves simultaneously struggling to raise children,
maintain a household, and hold a job. Similarly, divorce
reform that benefited wealthy women proved disastrous
to the poor. In the early 1970s feminists sought liberalized divorce legislation—including the quick, no-fault
divorce—in order to increase the life options available to
unhappy women. Successful in passing such legislation,
feminists watched in amazement as men took advantage
of the laws, gaining quick divorces and freeing themselves from alimony payments to former wives, leaving
often unprepared women to forage for jobs in an increasingly competitive market-place. Divorce rates climbed
82 percent during the decade. Usually saddled with the
task of supporting children and able to work only in
low-paying jobs, divorced women swelled the ranks of
the poor. By the 1980s, 60 percent of poor families were
headed by women, and the compound pressures of raising a family, low wages, and cutbacks in social services
made their situation even more dismal. By the end of
the decade Betty Friedan conceded that NOW's support
of liberalized divorce legislation—without provisions
for job training and child support—had been a "trap."
Such realizations forced feminists to reconsider women's
liberation as a movement directed towards limited goals
for a limited elite of Americans. Some feminists returned

to the broader social agenda of the late 1960s, which supplied the initial impetus for women's liberation. Historian Barbara Eherenreich called for a return to basics: "... that nothing short of equality will do *and* that in a society marred by injustice and cruelty, equality will never be good enough ... is still the best idea ... that women have ever had."

Discrimination Against Women Was Considered Normal in the 1960s

Gail Collins

In the following excerpt from her book *When Everything Changed*, Gail Collins describes the sex discrimination that was considered normal by girls who grew up during the 1960s. Since early childhood, they had been told that women were expected to marry and let their husbands deal with the outside world, and that they should not compete with men. She explains that there were scarcely any professional women or athletes. On television women were portrayed almost exclusively as homemakers; even though many low-income women did work, prestige lay in not having to do so. The few exciting careers, such as that of airline stewardess, lasted only a short time until the woman married and was required to quit. Men were presumed to be the money managers and married women could not get credit in their own names. Women unaccompanied by men were not accepted by establishments such as golf courses, some restaurants, and upscale bars, and there were many organizations open only to men. Gail Collins is an op-ed columnist for the *New York Times* and the author of several books.

The world around [girls in the 1960s] had been drumming one message into their heads since they were babies: women are meant to marry and let their husbands take care of all the matters relating to the outside world. They were not supposed to have adventures or compete with men for serious rewards. ("I think that when women are encouraged to be competitive too many of them become disagreeable," said Dr. Benjamin Spock, whose baby book had served as the bible for the postwar generation of mothers.) *Newsweek*, decrying a newly noticed phenomenon of dissatisfied housewives in 1960, identified the core of the issue: menstruation. "From the beginning of time, the female cycle has defined and confined woman's role," the newsmagazine wrote. "As [Sigmund] Freud was credited with saying: 'Anatomy is destiny.'" . . .

> Most girls grew up without ever seeing a woman doctor, lawyer, police officer, or bus driver.

Most girls grew up without ever seeing a woman doctor, lawyer, police officer, or bus driver. Jo Freeman, who went to Berkeley in the early '60s, realized only later that while she had spent four years "in one of the largest institutions of higher education in the world—and one with a progressive reputation," she had never once had a female professor. "I never even saw one. Worse yet, I didn't notice." If a young woman expressed interest in a career outside the traditional teacher/nurse/secretary, her mentors carefully shepherded her back to the proper path. . . .

Whenever things got interesting, women seemed to vanish from the scene. There was no such thing as a professional female athlete—even in schools, it was a given that sports were for boys. An official for the men-only Boston Marathon opined that it was "unhealthy for women to run long distances." . . .

The Portrayal of Women on Television

Nothing sent the message about women's limited options more forcefully than television. . . . The postwar generation that was entering adolescence in the 1960s had grown up watching *Howdy Doody*, the must-see TV for the first wave of baby boomers. *Howdy* was a raucous puppet show in which the human performers interspersed broad physical comedy with endless pitches for the sponsors' products. "But all the slapstick stopped when they brought out Princess Summerfall Winterspring," remembered Stephen Davis, a childhood fan whose father worked on the show. The princess, played by a teenage singer named Judy Tyler, was the only long-running female character in *Howdy Doody*'s crowded cast. The role had been created when a producer realized "we could sell a lot of dresses if only we had a girl on the show," and the princess spent most of her time expressing concern about plot developments taking place while she was offstage. Adults approved. "The harshness and crudeness which so many parents objected to in *Howdy Doody* now appears to have largely been a case of too much masculinity," said *Variety*. But the stuff that made kids love the show—the broad comedy and bizarre plots—was all on the male side of the equation. Princess Summerfall Winterspring sang an occasional song—and watched.

The more popular and influential television became, the more efficiently women were swept off the screen. In the 1950s, when the medium was still feeling its way, there were a number of shows built around women—mainly low-budget comedies such as *Our Miss Brooks*, *Private Secretary*, and *My Little Margie*. None of the main characters were exactly role models—Miss Brooks was a teacher who spent most of her time mooning over a hunky biology instructor, and Margie lived off her rich father. Still, the shows were unquestionably about them. And the most popular program of all was *I Love Lucy*, in which Lucille Ball was the focus of every plotline, ever striving to get out of her three-room apartment and into her husband Ricky's nightclub show.

But by 1960 television was big business, and if women were around at all, they were in the kitchen, where they decorously stirred a single pot on the stove while their husbands and children dominated the action. . . . When a script did turn its attention to the wife, daughter, or mother, it was frequently to remind her of her place and the importance of letting boys win. On *Father Knows Best*, younger daughter Kathy was counseled by her dad on how to deliberately lose a ball game. Teenage daughter Betty found happiness when she agreed to stop competing with a male student for a junior executive job at the local department store and settled for the more gender-appropriate task of modeling bridal dresses.

In dramatic series, women stood on the sidelines, looking worried. When [feminist] Betty Friedan asked why there couldn't be a female lead in *Mr. Novak*—which was, after all, a series about a high school teacher—she said the producer explained, "For drama, there has to be action, conflict. . . . For a woman to make decisions, to triumph over anything, would be unpleasant, dominant, masculine." Later in the decade, the original *Star Trek* series would feature a story about a woman so desperate to become a starship captain—a post apparently restricted to men—that she arranged to have her brain transferred into Captain Kirk's body. The crew quickly noticed that

> When a script did turn its attention to the wife, daughter, or mother, it was frequently to remind her of her place and the importance of letting boys win.

TV shows from the 1960s such as *Father Knows Best* showed women primarily in the kitchen while the husband and children dominated the plot. (Screen Gems/Getty Images.)

the captain was manicuring his nails at the helm and having hysterics over the least little thing.

Cowboy action series were the best-loved TV entertainment in 1960. Eleven of the top twenty-five shows were Westerns, and they underlined the rule that women did not have adventures, except the ones that involved getting kidnapped or caught in a natural disaster. . . .

TV created the impression that once married, a woman literally never left her house. Even if the viewers knew that this really wasn't true, many did accept the message that when matrimony began, working outside the home ended. In reality, however, by 1960 there were as many women working as there had been at the peak of World War II, and the vast majority of them were married. (Young single adult women were, as we'll see, as rare as female action heroes at this point in history.) More than 30 percent of American wives were holding down jobs, including almost 40 percent of wives with school-age children.

Yet to look at the way Americans portrayed themselves on television, in newspapers, and in magazines, you'd have thought that married women who worked were limited to a handful of elementary school teachers and the unlucky wives of sharecroppers and drunkards. . . .

Limited Job Options for Women

If all the working women were invisible, it was in part because of the jobs most of them were doing. . . . They were office workers—receptionists or bookkeepers, often part-time. They stood behind cash registers in stores, cleaned offices or homes. If they were professionals, they held—with relatively few exceptions—low-paying positions that had long been defined as particularly suited to women, such as teacher, nurse, or librarian. The nation's ability to direct most of its college-trained women into the single career of teaching was the foundation upon which the national public school system was built and a major reason American tax rates were kept low. . . .

Another reason the nation ignored the fact that so many housewives had outside jobs was that working women tended not to be well-represented among upper-income families. The male politicians, business executives, editors, and scriptwriters who set the tone for public discussion usually felt that wives not working was simply better. After the war, Americans had a powerful and understandable desire to settle down and return to normal. Since they were doing so in an era of incredible economic growth, it was easy to decide that stay-at-home housewives were part of the package. Women could devote all their energies to taking care of their children and husbands (politicians, businessmen, and editors

> A woman who worked to help support her struggling—or striving—family might want to downplay the fact rather than make her husband look inadequate.

included). If some of them wanted a break from domestic routine, they could volunteer to work on the PTA or, if they were wealthy enough, the charity fashion show. ("It is a tradition in the Guggenheimer family that all the men become lawyers and all the women work on committees," said a story in the *Times* about some well-to-do New Yorkers.) Men were supposed to be the breadwinners. A woman who worked to help support her struggling—or striving—family might want to downplay the fact rather than make her husband look inadequate. As late as 1970, a survey of women under 45 who had been or were currently married found that 80 percent believed "it is much better for everyone involved if the man is the achiever outside the home and the woman takes care of the home and family."

The limited options for women who did work, and the postwar propaganda about the glories of homemaking, convinced the young women who were graduating from high school and college in the early 1960s that once you married, the good life was the stay-at-home life. Prestige lay in having a husband who was successful enough to keep his wife out of the workplace. . . .

Employers happily took advantage of the assumption that female college graduates would work for only a few years before retiring to domesticity. They offered up a raft of theoretically glamorous short-term jobs that were intended to end long before the young women would begin to care about things like health care or pensions or even salaries. The sociologist David Riesman noted that instead of contemplating careers in fields such as business or architecture, "even very gifted and creative young women are satisfied to assume that on graduation they will get underpaid ancillary positions, whether as a *Time-Life* researcher or United Nations guide or publisher's assistant or reader, where they are seldom likely to advance to real opportunity."

The Aspiration to Be a Stewardess

First and foremost among these mini-career paths was being a stewardess. Girls in the postwar era had grown up reading books such as *Julie with Wings*, in which beautiful and spunky young women beat out the massive competition to become flight attendants. Along with teenage fiction about Cherry Ames, the inexhaustible nurse, the stewardess novels were virtually the only girls' career books around—unless you counted the girl detectives, who didn't seem to get paid for their efforts. Winning your "wings," readers learned, might require leaving behind an unimaginative boyfriend. . . .

> Women were vigorously discouraged from seeking jobs that men might have wanted.

Within a few chapters, the heroine of *Silver Wings for Vicki* had attracted two new boyfriends, met a movie star, and helped the police arrest a smuggler. In the real world, the job was a lot more mundane, but it was still virtually the only one a young woman could choose that offered the chance to travel. As a result, the airlines got more than a hundred applicants for every opening. . . .

Despite the fact that the American experience was built around women who ventured off to create homes in an unexplored continent, there had always been a presumption that a proper woman didn't move around too much, and there was certainly a conviction that sending a woman on a business trip raised far too many risks of impropriety.

Georgia Panter, a stewardess for United Airlines in 1960, noticed that except for the occasional family, her flights were populated only by men. One regular run, the "Executive Flight" from New York to Chicago, actually barred female passengers. The men got extra large steaks, drinks, and cigars—which the stewardesses were sup-posed to bend over and light.

Women had been eager participants in the early years of flying, when things were disorganized and open to all comers. But any hopes they had for gaining a foothold in commercial aviation were dashed when the Commerce Department, under pressure from underemployed male pilots, exiled women from the field by prohibiting them from flying planes carrying passengers in bad weather. Instead, they got the role of hostess. The airlines origi-nally hired nurses to serve as flight attendants, but by the postwar era, trained health-care workers were long gone and the airlines were looking for attractive, unmarried young women whose main duty would be to serve drinks and meals. . . .

The airlines tried to make sure their stewardesses didn't stay around long enough to become dissatisfied with their benefits or acquainted with their union. The average tenure . . . was about eighteen months, thanks to a rule requiring the women to quit if they got married. In an era that was breaking all records for early wed-dings, that was all it took to ensure very rapid turnover. If a stewardess was still on the job after three years, one United executive said in 1963, "I'd know we were getting the wrong kind of girl. She's not getting married." . . .

Widespread Discrimination Against Women

Women were vigorously discouraged from seeking jobs that men might have wanted. "Hell yes, we have a quota," said a medical school dean in 1961. "Yes, it's a small one. We do keep women out, when we can. We don't want them here—and they don't want them elsewhere, either, whether or not they'll admit it." Another spokesman for a medical school, putting a more benign spin on things, said, "Yes indeed, we do take women, and we do not want the one woman we take to be lonesome, so we take two per class." In 1960 women accounted for 6 percent of American doctors, 3 percent of lawyers, and less than 1 percent of engineers. Although more than half a million women worked for the federal government, they made up 1.4 percent of the civil-service workers in the top four pay grades. Those who did break into the male-dominated professions were channeled into low-profile specialties related to their sex. Journalists were shuttled off to the women's page, doctors to pediatric medicine, and lawyers to behind-the-scenes work such as real estate and insurance law.

Since it was perfectly legal to discriminate on the basis of sex, there was no real comeback when employers simply said that no women need apply. A would-be journalist named Madeleine Kunin, looking for her first reporting job, applied to the *Providence Journal* and was rebuffed by an editor, who said, "The last woman we hired got raped in the parking lot." She applied to the *Washington Post* and was told she was a finalist, then later was notified that "we decided to give the job to a man." After going to Columbia Journalism School for further training, she applied to the *New York Times*, hoping to become a copy-editor. "We don't have anything in the newsroom for you, but I could see if we could get you a waitressing job in the *Times* cafeteria," said the personnel director. . . .

> The idea that men were supposed to be in charge went beyond conventional wisdom; it was regarded by many as scientific fact.

When Ruth Bader Ginsburg, the future Supreme Court justice, went to Harvard Law School, the dean held a dinner for the handful of women in the class. He jovially opened up the conversation by asking them "to explain what we were doing in law school taking a place that could be held by a man."

Once hired, women had virtually no hope of moving up. A report on women in management by *Harvard*

Business Review in the 1960s said there were so few such women that "there is scarcely anything to study." The idea that men were supposed to be in charge went beyond conventional wisdom; it was regarded by many as scientific fact. A federally funded study of college students' career objectives concluded that the typical coed "most easily finds her satisfaction in fields where she supports and often underwrites the male, such as secretarial work or nursing, or in volunteer work which is not paid and is clearly valued by the sentimental side of community attitudes." . . .

Men, in their capacity as breadwinners, were presumed to be the money managers on the home front as well as in business, and women were cut out of almost everything having to do with finances. Credit cards were issued in the husband's name. Loans were granted based on the husband's wage-earning ability, even if the wife had a job, under the theory that no matter what the woman said she planned to do, she would soon become pregnant and quit working. . . .

Even when a woman was living on her own and supporting herself, she had trouble convincing the financial establishment that she could be relied upon to pay her bills. The *New York Times* was still reporting horror stories in 1972, such as that of a suburban mother who was unable to rent an apartment until she got the lease cosigned by her husband—a patient in a mental hospital. A divorced woman, well-to-do and over forty, had to get her father to cosign her application for a new co-op. Divorced women had a particular problem getting credit, in part because of a widely held belief that a woman who could not keep her marriage together might not keep her money under control, either. (Insurance companies held to the same line of reasoning when it came to writing policies for car owners, theorizing that a woman who broke the marital bonds would also break the speed limit.) . . .

When women ventured into the outside world, they often felt tentative, unsure of their welcome. And it was no wonder. The Executive Flight to Chicago was not the only service that barred them at the gate. The world was full of men's clubs, men's gyms, and men's lounges, where the business of business was conducted. Even places that were theoretically open to the public reserved the right to discriminate. The public golf course in Westport, Connecticut, would not allow women to play during prime weekend hours, claiming that men deserved the best spots because they had to work during the week. Heinemann's Restaurant in Milwaukee banned women from the lunch counter because "men needed faster service than women because they have important business to do." Many upscale bars refused to serve women, particularly if they were alone, under the theory that they must be prostitutes.

Early in the 1960s, a freelance writer from New York, traveling to Boston to interview a psychologist for a book she was working on, stopped by the Ritz-Carlton Hotel and ordered a drink at the bar. "We do not serve women," the bartender said, and whisked her off to a little lounge off the women's restroom, where he brought her the whiskey sour. It was a moment Betty Friedan recalled with humiliation decades later, long after she helped spark a movement that made sure nobody ever got consigned to that lounge again.

The National Organization for Women Aims to Change Women's Status

Betty Friedan

The following is the original statement of purpose adopted during the formation of the National Organization for Women (NOW), which successfully lobbied for legislation to reduce discrimination against women. It declares that changes in society are urgently needed if women are to develop their full human potential; that civil rights laws should apply to sex discrimination; that it should not be assumed that women must retire from the workplace to raise their children; and that higher education

is as necessary for girls as it is for boys. It also states that
all responsibilities should be shared equally within marriage;
that women must exercise their political rights and refuse to
be segregated by sex in political organizations; and that the
image of women presented by mass media must be changed.
Betty Friedan, the author of the statement, was the founder and
first president of NOW. Her 1963 book *The Feminine Mystique*
is generally regarded as having started the women's liberation
movement of the 1960s and 1970s.

W e, men and women who hereby constitute
ourselves as the National Organization for
Women [NOW], believe that the time has
come for a new movement toward true equality for all
women in America, and toward a fully equal partnership of the sexes, as part of the world-wide revolution of
human rights now taking place within and beyond our
national borders.

The purpose of NOW is to take
action to bring women into full
participation in the mainstream of
American society now, exercising
all the privileges and responsibilities
thereof in truly equal partnership
with men.

> "The time has come to con-
> front . . . the conditions that
> now prevent women from enjoy-
> ing the equality of opportunity
> and freedom of choice which is
> their right.

We believe the time has come to
move beyond the abstract argument,
discussion and symposia over the
status and special nature of women
which has raged in America in recent years; the time has
come to confront, with concrete action, the conditions
that now prevent women from enjoying the equality of
opportunity and freedom of choice which is their right,
as individual Americans, and as human beings.

NOW is dedicated to the proposition that women,
first and foremost, are human beings, who, like all other
people in our society, must have the chance to develop

their fullest human potential. We believe that women can achieve such equality only by accepting to the full the challenges and responsibilities they share with all other people in our society, as part of the decision-making mainstream of American political, economic and social life.

We organize to initiate or support action, nationally, or in any part of this nation, by individuals or organizations, to break through the silken curtain of prejudice and discrimination against women in government, industry, the professions, the churches, the political parties, the judiciary, the labor unions, in education, science, medicine, law, religion and every other field of importance in American society.

Changes in Society

Enormous changes taking place in our society make it both possible and urgently necessary to advance the unfinished revolution of women toward true equality, now. With a life span lengthened to nearly 75 years it is no longer either necessary or possible for women to devote the greater part of their lives to child-rearing; yet childbearing and rearing—which continues to be a most important part of most women's lives—still is used to justify barring women from equal professional and economic participation and advance.

Today's technology has reduced most of the productive chores which women once performed in the home and in mass-production industries based upon routine unskilled labor. This same technology has virtually eliminated the quality of muscular strength as a criterion for filling most jobs, while intensifying American industry's need for creative intelligence. In view of this new industrial revolution created by automation in the mid-twentieth century, women can

> Women can and must participate in old and new fields of society in full equality.

and must participate in old and new fields of society in full equality—or become permanent outsiders.

Despite all the talk about the status of American women in recent years, the actual position of women in the United States has declined, and is declining, to an alarming degree throughout the 1950's and 60's. Although 46.4% of all American women between the ages of 18 and 65 now work outside the home, the overwhelming majority—75%—are in routine clerical, sales, or factory jobs, or they are household workers, cleaning women, hospital attendants. About two-thirds of Negro women workers are in the lowest paid service occupations. Working women are becoming increasingly—not less—concentrated on the bottom of the job ladder. As a consequence, full-time women workers today earn on the average only 60% of what men earn, and that wage gap has been increasing over the past twenty-five years in every major industry group. In 1964, of all women with a yearly income, 89% earned under $5,000 a year; half of all full-time year round women workers earned less than $3,690; only 1.4% of full-time year round women workers had an annual income of $10,000 or more.

Further, with higher education increasingly essential in today's society, too few women are entering and finishing college or going on to graduate or professional school. Today, women earn only one in three of the B.A.'s and M.A.'s granted, and one in ten of the Ph.D.'s.

In all the professions considered of importance to society, and in the executive ranks of industry and government, women are losing ground. Where they are present it is only a token handful. Women comprise less than 1% of federal judges; less than 4% of all lawyers; 7% of doctors. Yet women represent 51% of the U.S. population. And, increasingly, men are replacing women in the top positions in secondary and elementary schools, in social work, and in libraries—once thought to be women's fields.

Sex Discrimination

Official pronouncements of the advance in the status of women hide not only the reality of this dangerous decline, but the fact that nothing is being done to stop it. The excellent reports of the President's Commission on the Status of Women and of the State Commissions have not been fully implemented. Such Commissions have power only to advise. They have no power to enforce their recommendation; nor have they the freedom to organize American women and men to press for action on them. The reports of these commissions have, however, created a basis upon which it is now possible to build. Discrimination in employment on the basis of sex is now prohibited by federal law, in Title VII of the Civil Rights Act of 1964. But although nearly one-third of the cases brought before the Equal Employment Opportunity Commission during the first year dealt with sex discrimination and the proportion is increasing dramatically, the Commission has not made clear its intention to enforce the law with the same seriousness on behalf of women as of other victims of discrimination. Many of these cases were Negro women, who are the victims of double discrimination of race and sex. Until now, too few women's organizations and official spokesmen have been willing to speak out against these dangers facing women. Too many women have been restrained by the fear of being called "feminist." There is no civil rights movement to speak for women, as there has been for Negroes and other victims of discrimination. The National Organization for Women must therefore begin to speak.

WE BELIEVE that the power of American law, and the protection guaranteed by the U.S. Constitution to the civil rights of all individuals, must be effectively applied and enforced to isolate and remove patterns of sex discrimination, to ensure equality of opportunity in employment and education, and equality of civil and political rights and responsibilities on behalf of women, as well as for Negroes and other deprived groups.

We realize that women's problems are linked to many broader questions of social justice; their solution will require concerted action by many groups. Therefore, convinced that human rights for all are indivisible, we expect to give active support to the common cause of equal rights for all those who suffer discrimination and deprivation, and we call upon other organizations committed to such goals to support our efforts toward equality for women.

WE DO NOT ACCEPT the token appointment of a few women to high-level positions in government and industry as a substitute for serious continuing effort to recruit and advance women according to their individual abilities. To this end, we urge American government and industry to mobilize the same resources of ingenuity and command with which they have solved problems of far greater difficulty than those now impeding the progress of women.

WE BELIEVE that this nation has a capacity at least as great as other nations, to innovate new social institutions which will enable women to enjoy the true equality of opportunity and responsibility in society, without conflict with their responsibilities as mothers and homemakers. In such innovations, America does not lead the Western world, but lags by decades behind many European countries. We do not accept the traditional assumption that a woman has to choose between marriage and motherhood, on the one hand, and serious participation in industry or the professions on the other. We question the present expectation that all normal women will retire from job or profession for 10 or 15 years to devote their full time

> We do not accept the traditional assumption that a woman has to choose between marriage and motherhood . . . and serious participation in industry or the professions.

> We believe that it is as essential for every girl to be educated to her full potential of human ability as it is for every boy.

to raising children, only to reenter the job market at a relatively minor level. This, in itself, is a deterrent to the aspirations of women, to their acceptance into management or professional training courses, and to the very possibility of equality of opportunity or real choice, for all but a few women. Above all, we reject the assumption that these problems are the unique responsibility of each individual woman, rather than a basic social dilemma which society must solve. True equality of opportunity and freedom of choice for women requires such practical and possible innovations as a nationwide network of child-care centers, which will make it unnecessary for women to retire completely from society until their children are grown, and national programs to provide retraining for women who have chosen to care for their children full-time.

WE BELIEVE that it is as essential for every girl to be educated to her full potential of human ability as it is for every boy—with the knowledge that such education is the key to effective participation in today's economy and that, for a girl as for a boy, education can only be serious where there is expectation that it will be used in society. We believe that American educators are capable of devising means of imparting such expectations to girl students. Moreover, we consider the decline in the proportion of women receiving higher and professional education to be evidence of discrimination. This discrimination may take the form of quotas against the admission of women to colleges, and professional schools; lack of encouragement by parents, counselors and educators; denial of loans or fellowships; or the traditional or arbitrary procedures in graduate and professional training geared in terms of men, which inadvertently discriminate against women. We believe that the same serious attention must be given to high school dropouts who are girls as to boys.

Betty Friedan met with the Pope on October 20, 1973, to urge the Catholic Church to "come to terms with the full personhood of women." **(AP Photo.)**

Partnership Between the Sexes

WE REJECT the current assumptions that a man must carry the sole burden of supporting himself, his wife, and family, and that a woman is automatically entitled to lifelong support by a man upon her marriage, or that marriage, home and family are primarily [a] woman's world and responsibility—hers, to dominate—his to support. We believe that a true partnership between the sexes demands a different concept of marriage, an equitable sharing of the responsibilities of home and children and of the economic burdens of their support. We believe that proper recognition should be given to the economic and social value of homemaking and child-care. To these ends, we will seek to open a reexamination of laws and mores governing marriage and divorce, for we believe that the current state of "half-equity" between the sexes discriminates against both men and women, and is the cause of much unnecessary hostility between the sexes.

WE BELIEVE that women must now exercise their political rights and responsibilities as American citizens. They must refuse to be segregated on the basis of sex into separate-and-not-equal ladies' auxiliaries in the political parties, and they must demand representation according to their numbers in the regularly constituted party committees—at local, state, and national levels—and in the informal power structure, participating fully in the selection of candidates and political decision-making, and running for office themselves.

IN THE INTERESTS OF THE HUMAN DIGNITY OF WOMEN, we will protest, and endeavor to change, the false image of women now prevalent in the mass media, and in the texts, ceremonies, laws, and practices of our major social institutions. Such images perpetuate contempt for women by society and by women for themselves. We are similarly opposed to all policies and practices—in church, state, college, factory, or office—which, in the guise of protectiveness, not only deny opportunities but also foster in women self-denigration, dependence, and evasion of responsibility, undermine their confidence in their own abilities and foster contempt for women.

NOW WILL HOLD ITSELF INDEPENDENT OF ANY POLITICAL PARTY in order to mobilize the political power of all women and men intent on our goals. We will strive to ensure that no party, candidate, president, senator, governor, congressman, or any public official who betrays or ignores the principle of full equality between the sexes is elected or appointed to office. If it is necessary to mobilize the votes of men and women who believe in our cause, in order to win for women the final right to be fully free and equal human beings, we so commit ourselves.

WE BELIEVE THAT women will do most to create a new image of women by acting now, and by speaking out in behalf of their own equality, freedom, and human dignity—not in pleas for special privilege, nor in enmity toward men, who are also victims of the current, half-equality between the sexes—but in an active, self-respecting partnership with men. By so doing, women will develop confidence in their own ability to determine actively, in partnership with men, the conditions of their life, their choices, their future and their society.

Civil Rights and Antiwar Activists Work Toward Women's Liberation

Gloria Steinem

In the following viewpoint, one of the most prominent advocates of women's liberation reports on the early stages of the movement, addressing readers who are not familiar with it. She describes the activities of some of the radical women's groups and how the members of these organizations became involved because of the unequal position they had held in groups that opposed the Vietnam War. She points out that less-radical middle-class women are joining the movement to protest discrimination in the workplace. The next step, she says, may be the involvement of poor women, which would allow the movement to grow strong enough to have political power. This will mean a time of conflict, especially since some women do not like having their traditional role questioned. But in the end, women's liberation will be good not only for women but for men, she says. Gloria Steinem is a writer, lecturer, editor, and feminist activist. She cofounded *Ms.* magazine and has authored several books.

SOURCE. Gloria Steinem, "After Black Power, Women's Liberation," *New York Magazine,* April 4, 1969. Copyright © 1969 by Gloria Steinem. All rights reserved. Reproduced by permission.

Once upon a time—say, ten or even five years ago—a Liberated Woman was somebody who had sex before marriage and a job afterward. Once upon the same time, a Liberated Zone was any foreign place lucky enough to have an American army in it. Both ideas seem antiquated now, and for pretty much the same reason: Liberation isn't exposure to the American values of Mom-and-apple-pie anymore (not even if Mom is allowed to work in an office and vote once in a while); it's the escape from them.

For instance:

Barnard girls move quietly, unlasciviously into the men's dorms at Columbia; a student sleep-in to protest the absence of "rational communities"—co-ed dorms like those already springing up at other universities.

Wives and mothers march around the Hudson Street alimony jail with posters announcing they don't *want* alimony.

A coven of 13 members of WITCH (the Women's International Terrorist Conspiracy from Hell, celebrating witches and gypsies as the first women resistance fighters) demonstrates against that bastion of white male supremacy: Wall Street. The next day, the market falls five points.

More witches and some black-veiled brides invade the Bridal Fair at Madison Square Garden. They carry signs ("Confront the Whore-makers," "Here Comes the Bribe"), sing, shout, release white mice in the audience of would-be brides, and generally scare the living daylights out of exhibitors who are trying to market the conventional delights of bridal gowns, kitchen appliances, package-deal honeymoon trips and heart-shaped swimming pools.

What Do Women Want?

At the end of the Columbia strike, the student-run Liberation School offers a course on women as an oppressed class. Discussions include the parallel myths about women and Negroes (that both have smaller brains than white men, childlike natures, natural "goodness," limited rationality, supportive roles to white men, etc.); the paternalistic family system as prototype for capitalistic society (see [Karl] Marx and [Friedrich] Engels); the conclusion that society can't be restructured until the relationship between the sexes is restructured. Men are kept out of the class, but it is bigger and lasts longer than any other at the school.

Redstockings, an action group in the Women's Liberation Movement, sponsors a one-act play about abortion by the New Feminist Theatre (whose purpose it is to point out how many plays are anti-woman and how tough it is for women playwrights, directors, producers), plus two hours of personal and detailed testimony—in public—by girls who have had abortions and Tell It

Gloria Steinem, seen in her New York apartment in March 1970, is one of the heroes of the women's liberation movement. (AP Photo.)

Like It Is, from humor through sadism. Nobody wants to reform the abortion laws; they want to repeal them. Completely.

What do women want? The above events are in no way connected to the Bloomingdale-centered, ask-not-what-I-can-do-for-myself-ask-what-my-husband-can-do-for-me ladies of Manhattan, who are said by sociologists to be "liberated." Nor do the house-bound matriarchs of Queens and the Bronx get much satisfaction out of reading about feminist escapades. On the contrary, the whole thing alienates them by being a) radical and b) young.

The women behind it, and influenced by it, usually turn out to be white, serious, well-educated girls; the same sort who have labored hard in what is loosely known as the Movement [the New Left Movement, which was composed of antiestablishment activists who opposed the Vietnam War], from the Southern sit-ins of nine years ago to the current attacks on the military-industrial-educational complex. They have been jailed, beaten and Maced side-by-side with their social-activist male counterparts. (It's wonderful to see how quickly police from Selma to Chicago get over a reluctance to hit women.) They have marched on Senate committees, Pentagon hawks, their own college presidents and the Chase Manhattan Bank. But once back in the bosom of SDS [Students for a Democratic Society], they found themselves typing and making coffee.

"When it comes to decision-making or being taken seriously in meetings," said one revolutionary theorist from Berkeley, "we might as well join the Young Republicans."

Igniting Women's Liberation

Such grumbling noises were being made aloud at Movement meetings as early as five years ago but women were ridiculed or argued down by men (as well as some "Uncle

Tom" women [women considered too sympathetic to traditional customs]). Eventually, they were assured, "the woman question" would come up on the list of radical priorities—as decided on by radical men. Meanwhile, more backstage work, more mimeographing, more secondary role-playing around the revolutionary cells and apartment-communes. And, to be honest, more reluctance to leave the secondary role and lose male approval.

> Women began to 'rap' (talk, analyze, in radical-ese) about their essential second-classness, forming women's caucuses inside the [New Left] Movement.

Finally, women began to "rap" (talk, analyze, in radical-ese) about their essential second-classness, forming women's caucuses inside the Movement in much the same way Black Power groups had done. And once together they made a lot of discoveries: that they shared more problems with women of different classes, for instance, than they did with men of their own; that they liked and respected each other (if women don't want to work with women, as Negroes used to reject other Negroes, it's usually because they believe the myth of their own inferiority); and that, as black militants kept explaining to white liberals, "You don't get radicalized fighting other people's battles."

At the SDS Convention in 1967, women were still saying such integrationist things as "The struggle for the liberation of women must be part of the larger fight for freedom." Many Movement women still are. But members of groups like the Southern Student Organizing Committee and New York Radical Women (a loose coalition of various radical groups whose representatives meet once a month) withdrew to start concentrating on their own problems. They couldn't become black or risk jail by burning their draft cards, but they could change society from the bottom up by radicalizing (engaging with basic truth) the consciousness of women; by going into the streets on such women's issues as abortion, free childcare centers, and a final break with the 19th-century definition of females as sex objects whose main function is to service men and their children.

All this happened not so much by organization as contagion. What has come to be known in the last two years or so as the Women's Liberation Movement (WLM) is no more pin-downable than the Black Power Movement; maybe less so, because white groups tend to be less structured, more skittish about leadership than black ones. Nonetheless, when the WLM had its first national conference last fall, women from 20 states and Canada showed up on a month's notice. A newsletter, *Voice of the Women's Liberation Movement* is published in Chicago. WLM-minded groups are springing up on dozens of campuses where they add special student concerns to their activities: professors who assume women aren't "serious" about careers; advisers who pressure girls toward marriage or traditionally feminine jobs (would-be Negro doctors are told to be veterinarians, would-be women doctors are told to be nurses); and faculties or administrations where few or no women are honored in authority.

In New York, WITCH is probably the most colorful outcropping of the WLM. It got started when women supporters of men being investigated by the House Un-American Activities Committee [HUAC] decided that a witch-hunt should have witches, and dressed up for HUAC hearings accordingly. (In the words of WITCH, "We are WITCH. We are WOMAN. We are LIBERATION. WE are WE. The hidden history of women's liberation began with witches and gypsies . . . the oldest guerrillas and resistance fighters, the first practicing abortionists and distributors of contraceptive herbs. WITCH implies the destruction of passivity, consumerism and commodity fetishism . . . the routine of daily life is the theatre of struggle.") It was the Witch Guerrilla Theatre that hexed Wall Street, and later, as part of a technique called "violating the reality structure," it "freaked out at a Wellesley Alumnae Fund-raising Bridge Party."

Quieter groups seem to be forming everywhere, from the New Women in Manhattan to The Feminists in Oceanside. Redstockings, the most publically active at the moment, has recapitulated the whole WLM in its short history. Women activists rebelled against their subordinate position, but still tried to work within the Movement until a peace-and-liberation protest at Nixon's Inaugural, where girls spoke and were booed by their own fellow radicals. After that moment of truth, they reformed as part of "an independent revolutionary movement, potentially representing half the population. We intend to make our own analysis of the system. . . . Although we may cooperate with radical men on matters of common concern . . . our demand for freedom involves not only the overthrow of capitalism, but the destruction of the patriarchal system."

> The WLM is growing so rapidly that even its most cheerful proselytizers are surprised.

Spreading Support

If all this sounds far-out, Utopian, elitist, unnecessary or otherwise unlikely to be the next big thing in revolutions, consider two facts: 1) the WLM is growing so rapidly that even its most cheerful proselytizers are surprised, spreading not only along the infra-structure of the existing co-ed Movement, but into a political territory where anti-Vietnam petitions have rarely been seen; and 2) there are a couple of mass movements, from highly organized through just restless, that the WLM might merge with, becoming sort of a revolutionary vanguard.

The older, middle-class women come first, the ones who tried hard to play subordinate roles in the suburbs according to the post-war-baby-boom-women's magazine idyll but found Something Missing. Betty Friedan, who explained their plight clearly and compassionately in *The Feminine Mystique*, named that Something: rewarding work. But when these women went out to find jobs, they found a lot of home-truths instead.

For instance, there is hardly a hierarchy in the country—business, union, government, educational, religious, whatever—that doesn't discriminate against women above the secretarial level. Women with some college education earn less than men who get as far as the eighth grade. The median income of white women

> "There is hardly a hierarchy in the country—business, union, government, educational, religious, whatever—that doesn't discriminate against women above the secretarial level."

employed full time is less than that of white men *and* Negro men. The gap between women's pay and men's pay gets greater every year, even though the number of women in the labor force increases (they are now a third of all workers). Forty-three states have "protection legislation" limiting the hours and place a woman can work; legislation that is, as Governor [of New York Nelson] Rockefeller admitted last year, "more often protective of men." The subtler, psychological punishments for stepping out of woman's traditional "service" role are considerable. (Being called "unfeminine," "a bad mother" or "a castrating woman," to name a traditional few.) And, to top it all off, the problem of servants or child care often proves insurmountable after others are solved.

In short, women's opportunities expanded greatly for about 15 years after they won the vote in 1920 (just as Negroes had more freedom during Reconstruction, before Jim Crow laws took over where slavery had left off), but they have been getting more limited ever since.

The middle-class, educated and disillusioned group gets larger with each college graduation. National Organization for Women (NOW)—founded in 1966 by Betty

Friedan, among others, "to bring women into full participation in the mainstream of American society *now*, exercising all the privileges and responsibilities thereof in truly equal partnership with men"—is a very effective voice of this group, concentrating on such reforms as getting irrelevant sex-designations out of Help Wanted ads and implementing Equal Employment Opportunity laws.

> It's the women who staff and win elections, and they may finally balk at working for only men.

If the WLM can feel solidarity with the hated middle class, and vice versa, then an alliance with the second mass movement—poor women of all colors—should be no problem. They are already organized around welfare problems, free daycare centers, for mothers who must work, and food prices. For them, equal pay, unequal training and sex discrimination for jobs (not to mention the woman-punishing rules of welfare) exact a daily price: Of all the families living below the poverty level, 40 per cent are headed by women.

A lot of middle-class and radical-intellectual women are already working with the poor on common problems, but viewing them as social. If the "consciousness-raising" programs of the WLM work, they'll see them as rallying points for women *qua* [by virtue of being] women. And that might forge the final revolutionary link. Rumblings are already being heard inside the Democratic Party in New York. It's the women who staff and win elections, and they may finally balk at working for only men—not very qualified men at that—in the mayoral primary.

A Time of Upheaval

There is plenty of opposition to this kind of thinking, from women as well as men. Having one's traditional role questioned is not a very comfortable experience; perhaps especially for women, who have been able to remain children, and to benefit from work they did not and could not do. Marriage wouldn't go straight down the drain, as traditionalists keep predicting. Women's liberation might just hurry up some sort of companionate marriage that seems to be developing anyway.

But there is bound to be a time of, as social anthropologist Lionel Tiger puts it, "increased personal acrimony," even if the revolution fails and women go right back to darning socks. (Masculinity doesn't depend on the subservience of others, but it will take us a while to find that out.) It might be helpful to men—and good for women's liberation—if they just keep repeating key phrases like, "No more guilt, No more alimony, Fewer boring women, Fewer bitchy women, No more tyrants with all human ambition confined to the home, No more 'Jewish mothers' transferring ambition to children, No more women trying to be masculine because it's a Man's World . . ." (and maybe one more round of "No more alimony") until the acrimony has stopped.

Because the idea is, in the long run, that women's liberation will be men's liberation, too.

Women's Liberation Activists Protest the Miss America Pageant

Linda Napikoski

Among the most widely publicized events of the women's liberation movement was the "Miss America Protest" on September 7, 1968. Feminist activists opposed the annual pageant because they felt women should not be judged solely on external beauty or have the ambition to win on that basis, and because they considered it racist. They also felt that it supported the Vietnam War because the winner was sent there to entertain the troops. Demonstrators called the pageant a "cattle auction" and nominated a sheep for Miss America, which they crowned during the live television broadcast. However, they did not burn any bras, as is commonly believed, although they threw some in a trash can along with other things they considered "items of oppression." Linda Napikoski is

SOURCE. Linda Napikoski, "Feminists at the Miss America Pageant," About.com, 2011. Copyright © 2011 Linda Napikoski (http://womenshistory.about.com). Used with permission of About .com, which can be found online at www.about.com. All rights reserved.

a journalist with a law degree who specializes in women's rights issues. She lives in Andong, Korea.

The Miss America Pageant that took place on September 7, 1968, was no ordinary pageant. Hundreds of feminist activists showed up on the Atlantic City Boardwalk to enact their "Miss America Protest." They distributed publicity materials titled "No More Miss America!"

The group behind the Miss America Protest was New York Radical Women. Prominent feminists who participated included Carol Hanisch, who originally had the idea to protest the pageant, as well as Robin Worcaji and Kathie Sarachild.

What Was Wrong with Miss America?

The women who came to the Miss America Protest had several complaints about the pageant:

- It judges women on impossible standards of beauty. The protesters called the standards "ludicrous."
- The pageant objectifies women and thereby harms all women.
- The protesters disliked the hypocrisy of the pageant, specifically the double standard of the Madonna [virginal saint]/whore fantasy, in which men irrationally demand that women be innocent and beautiful, while also satisfying the men's lust.

The feminists had other political disagreements with the pageant as well.

- They considered the pageant racist, for never having had a black Miss America.
- The activists opposed the Vietnam War and felt the pageant supported it by sending the Miss America

winner to Vietnam to entertain the troops.

- There was a blatant inequality in encouraging girls to grow up to become Miss America. The standard line in the United States to any boy was that he could grow up to be president. Why not women? Why was Miss America supposed to be their equivalent dream?

The women at the Miss America Protest also criticized the consumer aspect of the pageant and the sponsors who used the contestants to promote their products. At the protest, the feminists of New York Radical Women announced a boycott of the companies that sponsored the pageant.

"Cattle Auction"

The Miss America Protest began in the afternoon on the boardwalk. There, at least 150 women marched with signs of protest. Some of their slogans called the pageant a cattle auction, for parading women around to judge them on their looks, the way men would judge cattle to decide the animals' worth.

The protesters nominated a sheep for Miss America and even crowned a live sheep on the boardwalk.

> The protest received media attention, which in turn attracted more women to the Women's Liberation movement.

At the end of the evening, when the winner was crowned, several of the protesters who had sneaked inside unfurled a banner from the balcony that read "Women's Liberation."

Miss America was a highly anticipated and widely watched event in 1968, so much of the nation tuned in to the live broadcast. The protest received media attention, which in turn attracted more women to the Women's Liberation movement. The protesters asked the media to send female reporters to cover their demonstration, and demanded that if there were any arrests that they only be made by women police officers.

A member of the New York Radical Women group, protesting the 1968 Miss America pageant, drops a bra into a "freedom trash can." (**AP Photo.**)

Bras on Fire?

The Miss America Protest apparently gave birth to one of the greatest myths of the women's rights movement: the myth of bra burning.

The protesters at the Miss America Pageant threw items of their oppression into a "freedom trash can." Among these items of oppression were girdles, high-heeled shoes, some bras, copies of *Playboy* magazine, and hair curlers. The women never lit these items on fire; throwing them out was the symbolism of the day. It has been reported that the women attempted to get a permit to burn the items but were denied because of the danger fire would pose to the wooden Atlantic City Boardwalk.

The intent to set them on fire may have been what sparked the rumor that bras actually were burned. There is no documented instance where 1960s feminists burned their bras, although the legend persists.

Feminists protested Miss America again in 1969, although the second protest was smaller and did not receive much attention. The Women's Liberation Movement continued to grow and develop, with more protests occurring and the more feminist groups being formed over the next few years. The Miss America Pageant still exists; the pageant moved from Atlantic City to Las Vegas in 2006.

Women Go on Strike for Equal Opportunities in Jobs and Education

David M. Dismore

The following article was originally published on the fortieth anniversary of the nationwide women's strike of 1970. That event marked the beginning of women's liberation as a national grassroots movement rather than mere activism on the part of radicals. The author tells what happened on that day, August 26, 1970, which marked the fiftieth anniversary of the Nineteenth Amendment that gave women the right to vote. The National Organization for Women (NOW) had proposed that women working at low-paid jobs, such as secretaries and waitresses, go "on strike" and march to protest discrimination, she says. Far more women showed up to march in New York than had been expected, and demonstrations were also held in other cities, showing that the movement was an idea whose time had come. David M. Dismore is a feminist history researcher and writes for *Ms.* magazine.

SOURCE. David M. Dismore, "When Women Went on Strike: Remembering Equality Day, 1970," *Ms. Blog*, August 26, 2010. Msmagazine.com. Copyright © 2010 by Ms. Magazine the World of Women. All rights reserved. Reproduced by permission.

Bold moves and high-risk strategies have been a feminist tradition since the days of Alice Paul and Susan B. Anthony. But on March 20, 1970, when Betty Friedan gave her farewell address as outgoing president of NOW and called for a nationwide women's strike on August 26 (the 50th anniversary of winning the vote), the other officers in the room were surprised, to put it mildly.

According to a *New York Times* article on March 21, 1970, Friedan (who is called "militant leader" in the headline) wanted "an instant revolution against sexual oppression" and proposed that:

> The women who are doing menial chores in the offices as secretaries put the covers on their typewriters and close their notebooks and the telephone operators unplug their switchboards, the waitresses stop waiting, cleaning women stop cleaning and everyone who is doing a job for which a man would be paid more stop. . . . And when it begins to get dark, instead of cooking dinner or making love, we will assemble and we will carry candles alight in every city to converge the visible power of women at city hall. . . . Women will occupy for the night the political decision-making arena and sacrifice a night of love to make the political meaning clear.

That was a tall order for a three-and-a-half-year-old organization like the National Organization for Women, with 3,033 members, 35 chapters and an annual budget of $38,000, to carry out. Formal organizations were surely just the tip of feminism's iceberg, however, and Betty was certain that somewhere out there were a lot of women who would march and protest if given a time and place to do so. But they had better show up, because every media outlet would see August 26, 1970 as *the* test of feminism's credibility and power.

NOW officially endorsed the idea, and three days later announced that the strike on August 26, 1970, would commemorate both the date that the 19th Amendment was ratified and "signal the start of a major political effort for the liberation of the women of the United States of America."

Though the three main purposes of the action were (a) repeal of antiabortion laws (b) establishment of child-care centers, and (c) equal opportunity in jobs and education, the media had a field day ridiculing a "women's strike,"

At a Washington, D.C., protest march for women's rights in 1970, women hang their signs on a statue of Admiral David G. Farragut. (**ES/AP Images.**)

with as many references to *Lysistrata* as your average Greek literature class. But the later stories often noted when and where a local rally or protest would be, so the word got out that this was more than a "strike" and there were many ways to show support for equality.

August 10 brought the first hint of actions to come. According to an Associated Press article the following day, about a hundred women went out to "liberate" the Statue of Liberty, unfurling a banner on her pedestal reading "Women of the World Unite" as a way of publicizing the upcoming strike and march. But while there were hints of a groundswell of support as the Big Day drew near, there was really no way of knowing whether the turnout would match the expectations.

"Equality Week" was literally kicked off in Boston by a karate demonstration on August 23, while an ad-hoc coalition of 52 groups finalized their plans for New York's events. The march down Fifth Avenue was still to be restricted to only one lane, a plan city authorities felt was more than adequate for the number of marchers they expected.

> "Not only were numerous feminist organizations represented, but even passersby who knew nothing of the march spontaneously joined in their first feminist action.

When August 26 arrived, the first planned events—from leafleting to guerrilla theatre—went off as scheduled, and as the day went on one could see women's rights banners hanging from windows. Finally, the moment of truth: How many would be at the assembly area to march?

It was a "sea of people"—far larger than anyone had dared hope. It easily rivaled, and according to some estimates exceeded, the largest suffrage marches the city had seen more than half a century before. Not only were numerous feminist organizations represented, but even passersby who knew nothing of the march spontaneously joined in their first feminist action. The assembly point filled to capacity, and as more kept arriving and trying to wedge their way in the marchers exploded into the street, tossing barriers aside as they took up every square inch of pavement from sidewalk to sidewalk. There were chants, buttons, signs ("Don't Iron While The Strike Is Hot") and props such as a giant typewriter chained to several marchers.

The rally at the end of the march was successful as well, with Bella Abzug, Gloria Steinem, Betty Friedan and many others telling politicians, press and other skeptics who didn't believe that American women had any meaningful discontent with the status quo, "We told you so."

The enthusiasm of that day spanned the nation, with marches and other events in 90 cities and 42 states. "Freedom Trash Cans" were set up from Syracuse, N.Y., to the Pentagon, where "objects of oppression" such as aprons and hair curlers were deposited (no husbands, however, despite many wry predictions.) In Miami, feminists smashed coffee cups to show that making coffee instead of policy was no longer enough for women in politics. In Los Angeles there was a march, rally and a tribute to living suffragists, plus lines of women dressed in white bearing banners like those of the "Silent Sentinels" who picketed President Wilson to prod him into supporting suffrage. There were "baby-ins" at offices by employed mothers to show the need for day care, and a plaque "consecrating" a site to a future statue of Susan B. Anthony was placed in a New York park to highlight the fact that the only statue of a female in the nation's largest city other than the Statue of Liberty was one of Alice in Wonderland.

There are few times when it can clearly be said that an idea or movement's time has come. For the Second Wave

> In Miami, feminists smashed coffee cups to show that making coffee instead of policy was no longer enough for women in politics.

of feminism to go from just 28 people meeting in a hotel room on June 29, 1966 to the nationwide outpouring of August 26, 1970 proves that this was one of those occasions. So Equality Day should really be a double celebration, honoring the events and pioneers of both 1920 and 1970, as the younger feminists of 2010 join veterans of the movement in the next stage of the battle for equality.

The Women's Liberation Movement Is Having an Impact on American Society

Isa Kapp

The following article from the United Nations magazine *UNESCO Courier* was written to tell readers worldwide about the women's liberation movement in the United States. The author explains the controversy over the Equal Rights Amendment and speculates about why women's rights has become a major issue at this particular time. It is not only because of injustice in job opportunities and pay, she says. Modern technology has lessened the work of homemaking so that it no longer gives women a sense of value; moreover, many found it unfulfilling after working in defense industries during World War II. The publication of *The Feminine Mystique* by Betty Frieden made some women suddenly conscious of the problem and led to lobbying for laws to ensure equality with men. However, younger women involved in civil rights activism want more social radical changes, and they constitute a vocal minority, she says. Isa Kapp was a literary critic who wrote for many prominent magazines.

Since the mid-1960s, a formidable conglomeration of organizations, programmes and manifestoes known as the Women's Liberation Movement has erupted in the United States with extraordinary force. Dedicated to the assertion of equal rights in all fields—work, education, law—the movement has grown at an astonishing rate, and by now hundreds of thousands of women have participated in at least one of its groups or activities.

There have been mass demonstrations and energetic campaigns directed at opening up a wider range of life alternatives for women, and an ardent struggle for the enactment of the Equal Rights Amendment ("Equality of rights under the law shall not be denied or abridged by the United States or by any State on account of sex.")

Finally passed by Congress in 1972, after being introduced and ignored by the federal legislature each year since 1923, this constitutional amendment is still short by four states of the 38 required to ratify it, but its progress to this point represents a considerable success by the liberationists.

> The new movement has wielded enormous political strength—it has intimidated male legislators, changed laws, enjoyed increasing access to the media.

In addition, there has been a flood of books dealing with women's position in society, and several new feminist magazines have been launched. Most prominent of these is *Ms.*, which has a circulation of 400,000 and covers the political, cultural and personal of women.

The title is pronounced *miz*, a new "liberated" form of address which avoids identifying women on the basis of their marital status. A more recent entry into the journalistic competition is *womanSports*, published by tennis star Billie Jean King and her husband.

The new movement has wielded enormous political strength—it has intimidated male legislators, changed laws, enjoyed increasing access to the media. But impressive though its impact has been, it is not really a new phenomenon in American life.

Despite the feeling of many of its participants that they are engaged in a radical contemporary cause, the feminist movement actually goes far back in American history, to the early 19th century, when the "woman issue" was extensively debated in the national press, in political gatherings and from church pulpits. . . .

Why Now?

What is it that has just this past decade brought the vocal minority to such a crescendo of protest? This is, after all, the period when women in the U.S.A. have come to make up more than 40 per cent of the university population, when liberalized divorce laws, varied birth control methods, and technological improvements have guaranteed them tremendous personal freedom, when women on their own merit have achieved distinction in politics as members of Congress, mayors of cities, state legislators, and when the important New England state of Connecticut now has a woman governor.

So why, when women as a whole exert unprecedented influence both on family and public policy, have modern feminists been moved to characterize the female role in society as being an outrageously subservient one?

For one thing, they point to what they see as glaring inequities in the work world. Of the 35 million women employed in the United States a third are secretaries or clerks, and over a fifth are service workers, such as waitresses or domestics. They are poorly represented in the professions and in management.

WOMEN'S SUPPORT FOR EFFORTS TO STRENGTHEN WOMEN'S STATUS

Percent in favor of strengthening women's status.

	1970	1972	1974	1980	1985
Single	53%	62%	69%	75%	84%
Divorced/separated	61%	57%	68%	75%	84%
Married	38%	46%	55%	64%	70%
Widowed	36%	40%	49%	48%	61%
18 to 29	46%	56%	67%	74%	80%
30 to 39	40%	49%	70%	70%	76%
40 to 49	39%	42%	63%	60%	76%
50 and older	35%	41%	56%	55%	64%
Urban	47%	52%	64%	62%	
Rural	34%	40%	51%	46%	
White	37%	45%	55%	62%	72%
Black	60%	62%	67%	77%	78%
No high school	36%	42%	43%	54%	63%
High school	38%	43%	56%	63%	72%
College +	44%	57%	67%	73%	79%

Taken from: Ethel Klein, "The Diffusion of Consciousness in the United States and Western Europe," *The Women's Movements of the United States and Western Europe: Consciousness, Political Opportunity, and Public Policy*. Mary Fainsod Katzenstein and Carol McClurg Mueller, eds. Temple University Press, 1987. p 26. Original data source: 1985 Virginia Slims American Women's Opinion Poll.

The average yearly income of full-time female workers is less than two-thirds of the male average. (Of course, this differentiation is to some extent one of circumstance rather than of discrimination: women tend to leave jobs, for family reasons, before they reach the highest salary level, and men in blue-collar jobs tend to belong to unions that have won high wage rates.)

Further, when men and women do equal work, women often get lesser titles and lower pay. Women who are full professors earn an average of ten per cent less than men, and the disparities are even greater in other fields.

The women's movement cited additional grievances. Some states still discriminated against women in inheritance rights and in the control of their own property in marriage. Some universities still denied women equal access to professional schools or to scholarships. And some state laws still treated women more harshly than men for certain types of crimes.

There is no doubt that these are legitimate areas in which to demand reforms, but there were also larger cultural and social forces which accounted for the urgency and energy of the Women's Liberation Movement. In this view, modern woman is at the mercy, not so much of men, as of rapid social change—urbanization, science and technology.

In the predominantly rural society that America was up to around 1900, a wife and mother was often employed from early morning until late at night, baking bread, preparing meals, washing, sewing, knitting, and fetching water from the well. But today small mobile families have made the home less central and stable than it once was; and electric refrigerators, washing machines and frozen foods have relegated the female to the most minor chores of homemaking.

No wonder that she needs to recover her lost value and self-respect by seeking new roles in the outside world. Possessing leisure and often a college education, caught up in our current passion for questioning all traditional values and institutions, she has become a recruit for the revolution of rising expectations.

Yet all of these grievances simmered below the surface until the mid-1960s. There were hints of restiveness directly after World War II when thousands of women who had worked in defence industries relinquished their jobs to demobilized veterans, and discovered that full-time homemaking was an anticlimax after the status and excitement of going to work.

> The rumble of feminism was hardly audible in the 1950s, partly because most women were deeply relieved to have their men home from the battlefields.

In 1952, an English translation of *The Second Sex*, by the French philosopher Simone de Beauvoir, stoked the fires of intellectual rebellion. But despite these provocations, the rumble of feminism was hardly audible in the 1950s, partly because most women were deeply relieved to have their men home from the battlefields.

The Feminine Mystique

What brought all these dormant dissatisfactions to consciousness was the publication in 1963 of Betty Friedan's *The Feminine Mystique*. Based mainly on interviews with her classmates 15 years after graduation from a women's college, her book formulated what the author called "the problem that has no name," an unspoken discontent that prevailed among thousands of educated women.

Many of them had eagerly embarked upon marriage and domesticity in an effort to compensate for the loneliness of the war years, yet a decade later she found them tired and unfulfilled, victims of "the feminine mystique," the view which educators, the media and business conspired to impose: that motherhood and housekeeping were the most rewarding occupations for women.

Title IX

In 1972 a major advance in educational opportunities for women was made when Congress passed the Title IX of the Educational Amendments of 1972, an addition to the Civil Rights Act of 1964. Generally known simply as Title IX, this law reads: "No person in the United States shall, on the basis of sex, be excluded from participation in, be denied the benefits of, or be subjected to discrimination under any education program or activity receiving Federal financial assistance."

Twenty-five years later, in 1997, a report by the US Department of Education stated:

> Since its passage in 1972, Title IX has had a profound impact on helping to change attitudes, assumptions and behavior and consequently, our understanding about how sexual stereotypes can limit educational opportunities. As the First Circuit Court of Appeals noted in a recent Title IX case, "interest and ability rarely develop in a vacuum; they evolve as a function of opportunity and experience." Decision making in schools and in the labor market that relies on gender to assess what students and employees know and are able to do is both archaic and ineffective.

Against this notion Mrs. Friedan argued vehemently: "The only way for a woman, as for a man, to find herself, to know herself as a person, is by creative work of her own." The impact of her book was enormous—it sold one and a half million copies—and the women's liberation movement as it now exists in America must date itself from its publication.

In 1966, Betty Friedan formally launched the National Organization for Women (NOW), a moderate group that acted, for the first time in the United States, as a lobby to press for equality of women in all spheres. Its membership was composed mainly of professional women and middle-class housewives, its language was sober, and its goals were largely political and economic.

NOW's strong support was in good part responsible for the rapid passage by the U.S. Congress of the Equal Rights Amendment and its subsequent approval by 34 state legislatures; and for removing specification as to sex from the "help wanted" section of newspapers. It also worked for vigorous enforcement of the Equal Pay Act of 1963, and by 1974 more than $50 million in back wages had been awarded to over 100,000 female employees.

> Most American women still look for emotional security and gratification in their own families, and are not aware of any far-reaching exploitation by men.

But if it was relatively militant in terms of practical reforms, NOW did not seem to meet the emotional requirements of younger or lower-class women, who were in search of some more primary confrontation with men. A number of splinter groups and new organizations were formed, many of them calling for a total revaluation of male-female relations.

Some questioned such traditional institutions as the "nuclear family" (consisting of only parents and children); others even argued that marriage must be abolished because "it has the same effect the institution of slavery had." (The passionate rhetoric and often disruptive tactics of these radical groups were clearly borrowed from the civil rights movement which reached its peak of activism and success in the mid-1960s.)

In my opinion, most American women still look for emotional security and gratification in their own families, and are not aware of any far-reaching exploitation by men. Indeed a number of women might admit, if they are honest, that they themselves are often in the role of exploiter. And they might willingly accept the anthropological view that the family was created precisely for the protection of women and children during the periods of their helplessness.

Nevertheless, the feminist movement has acted as an intellectual spur. It has ensured public debate on a number of fundamental questions that have not, until now, received lively consideration. . . .

The Movement's Impact

The Women's Liberation Movement has clearly done an important service in bringing feminine discontents

Thousands of women, like these workers assembling the fuselage of a B-17 bomber, were employed during World War II and had to give up their jobs to returning veterans after the war. (Buyenlarge/ Getty Images.)

and desire for self-improvement into the arena of public discussion. By doing so it has changed the emotional ambience of male-female relationships and made them in some ways more resilient and elastic. The movement can also take credit for the rapid opening up of educational and career opportunities for women. To cite only two examples: between 1965 and 1973 female enrollment in medical schools nearly doubled and in law schools more than tripled.

Many inequalities, of course, still exist. Women still earn considerably less than men in all major occupations—at a time when more and more U.S. families are headed by women, many without incomes other than their salaries. While inequities are narrowing in education, women are not yet even near parity with men at the postgraduate level or in professional schools. Labour unions have been accused of resisting the admission of women to full equality in job-training and apprenticeship programmes.

In the effort to eliminate such grievances, the Women's Liberation Movement has been successful in gaining support from an increasing number of working-class women, as well as from a surprisingly large proportion of men who, in public opinion polls, show a greater approval of the movement's goals than women.

Without doubt, the next decade will see a growing movement of women into all occupations and areas of American life: in the professions, in politics, and in the academic world.

Even today, despite remnants of discrimination, a woman can choose how she wishes to order her life. She can devote herself to marriage, or pursue a career, or opt for both and derive considerable satisfaction from managing the practical difficulties this may present. She may decide on a part-time career and deliberately give precedence to home and motherhood.

Women are not homogeneous. Some are eager to make their way in the outside world, and some prefer not to compete with men. Perhaps for the first time in history, the variety of choices open to them will correspond to the variety of their impulses.

CHAPTER 2

Controversies Surrounding the Women's Liberation Movement

The Claims of the Women's Liberation Movement Are Unjustified

Murray Rothbard

In the following viewpoint, an economist expresses his disapproval of the women's liberation movement. He states that women are not oppressed and that this is shown by the fact that no men have bothered to contest the claim that they are. The movement, he says, is part of the "crackpot" activity of the New Left, although there is a somewhat less irrational faction that focuses on alleged economic discrimination against women. In his opinion, women earn less than men because they take time out to raise children and because their productivity is lower than men's. In answer to groups that blame capitalism for women's oppression, he points out that in the feudal, precapitalist society women were owned by their fathers and husbands;

Photo on previous page: After decades of controversy and struggles with their union, Fire Station Three, an all-woman firefighting company, opened in San Diego in 1996. (**Gilles Mingasson/Liaison/Getty Images.**)

capitalism set them free. That there are still few women in high positions is not because they are "brainwashed," as feminists claim, but because most women honestly prefer to be housewives and mothers. He argues that men, rather than women, are oppressed in society because they do most of the work. Murray Rothbard, an author and economist, was a central figure in the libertarian movement in the United States. He wrote more than twenty books.

It is high time, and past due, that someone blew the whistle on "Women's Liberation." Like the environment, women's lib is suddenly and raucously everywhere. It has become impossible to avoid being assaulted, day in and day out, by the noisy blather of the women's movement. Special issues of magazines, TV news programs, and newspapers have been devoted to this new-found "Problem"; and nearly two dozen books on women's lib are being scheduled for publication this year by major publishers. In all this welter of verbiage, not one article, not one book, not one program has dared to present the opposition case. The injustice of this one-sided tidal wave should be evident. Not only is it evident, but the lack of published opposition negates one of the major charges of the women's lib forces: that the society and economy are groaning under a monolithic male "sexist" tyranny. If the men are running the show, how is it that they do not even presume to print or present anyone from the other side? Yet the "oppressors" remain strangely silent, which leads one to suspect, as we will develop further below, that perhaps the "oppression" is on the other side.

In the meanwhile, the male "oppressors" are acting, in the manner of liberals everywhere, like scared, or guilt-ridden, rabbits. When the one hundred viragoes [loud, domineering women] of women's lib bullied their way into the head offices of the *Ladies' Home Journal*, did the harried editor-in-chief, John Mack Carter, throw these aggressors out on their collective ear, as he should have done? Did he, at the very least, abandon his office for the day and go home? No, instead he sat patiently for eleven hours while these harridans heaped abuse upon him and his magazine and his gender, and then meekly agreed to donate to them a special section of the *Journal*, along with $10,000 ransom. In this way, spineless male liberalism meekly feeds the appetite of the aggressors and paves the way for the next set of outrageous "demands." . . .

Why, in fact, this sudden upsurge of women's lib? Even the most fanatic virago of the women's movement concedes that this new movement has not emerged in response to any sudden clamping down of the male boot upon the collective sensibilities of the American female. Instead, the new uprising is part of the current degeneracy of the New Left, which, as its one-time partly libertarian politics, ideology, and organization have collapsed, has been splintering into absurd and febrile forms, from Maoism [a form of communism based on the teachings of Chinese leader Mao Zedong] to Weathermanship [tactics of the Weathermen, a radical left organization] to mad bombings to women's lib. The heady wine of "liberation" for every crackpot group has been in the air for some time, sometimes deserved but more often absurd, and now the New Left women have gotten into the act. We need not go quite so far as the recent comment of Professor Edward A. Shils, eminent sociologist at the University of Chicago, that he now expects a "dog liberation front," but it is hard to fault the annoyance behind his remark. . . .

Why Women Earn Less than Men

The current women's movement is divisible into two parts. The older slightly less irrational wing began in 1963 with the publication of Betty Friedan's *The Feminine Mystique* and her organization of NOW (the National Organization for Women). NOW concentrates on alleged economic discrimination against women. For example: the point that while the median annual wage for all jobs in 1968 was almost $7,700 for men, it only totaled $4,500 for women, 58 percent of the male figure. The other major point is the quota argument: that if one casts one's eye about various professions, top management positions, etc., the quota of women is far lower than their supposedly deserved 51 percent share of the total population. The quota argument may be disposed of rapidly; for it is a two-edged sword. If the low percentage of women in surgery, law, management, etc., is proof that the men should posthaste be replaced by females, then what are we to do with the Jews, for example, who shine far above their assigned quota in the professions, in medicine, in academia, etc.? Are they to be purged?

The lower average income for women can be explained on several grounds, none of which involve irrational "sexist" discrimination. One is the fact that the overwhelming majority of women work a few years and then take a large chunk of their productive years to raise children, after which they may or may not decide to return to the labor force. As a result, they tend to enter, or to find, jobs largely in those industries and in that type of work that does not require a long-term commitment to a career. Furthermore, they tend to find jobs in those occupations where the cost of training new people, or of losing old ones, is relatively low. These tend to be lower-paying occupations than those that require a long-term commitment or where costs of training or turnover are high. This general tendency to take out years for child raising also accounts for a good deal of the failure to promote women to higher-ranking and, therefore, higher-paying jobs and hence for the low female "quotas" in these areas. It is easy to hire secretaries who do not intend to make the job their continuing life work; it is not so easy to promote people up the academic or the corporate ladder who do not do so. How does a dropout for motherhood get to *be* a corporate president or a full professor?

While these considerations account for a good chunk of lower pay and lower ranked jobs for women, they do not fully explain the problem. In the capitalist market economy, women have full freedom of opportunity; irrational discrimination in employment tends to be minimal in the free market, for the simple reason that the employer also suffers from such discriminatory practice. In the free market, every worker tends to earn the value of his product, his "marginal productivity." Similarly, everyone tends to fill the job he can best accomplish, to work at his most productive efforts. Employers who persist in paying below a person's marginal product will hurt themselves by losing their best workers and hence losing profits for themselves. If women have persistently lower pay and poorer jobs, even after correcting for the motherhood-dropout, then the simple reason must be that their marginal productivity tends to be lower than men's.

It should be emphasized that, in contrast to the women's lib forces who tend to blame capitalism as well as male tyrants for centuries-old discrimination, it was precisely capitalism and the "capitalist revolution" of the eighteenth and nineteenth centuries that freed women from male oppression and set each woman free to find her best level. It was the feudal and precapitalist, pre-market society that was marked by male oppression; it was that society where women were chattels of their fathers and husbands, where they could own no property of their own, etc. Capitalism set women free to find their own level, and the result is what we have today. The women's libs retort that women possess the full potential of equality of output and productivity with men, but that

> The overwhelming majority of women . . . do feel that their sole careers are those of housewife and mother.

they have been browbeaten during centuries of male oppression. But the conspicuous lack of rising to the highest posts under capitalism still remains. There are few women doctors, for example. Yet medical schools nowadays not only don't discriminate against women, they bend over backwards to accept them (that is, they discriminate in their favor); yet the proportion of women doctors is still not noticeably high.

Most Women Prefer to Be Homemakers

Here the female militants fall back on another argument: that centuries of being "brainwashed" by a male-dominated culture have made most women passive, accepting their allegedly inferior role, and even liking and enjoying their major role as homemakers and child raisers. And the real problem for the raucous females, of course, is that the overwhelming majority of women do embrace the "feminine mystique," do feel that their sole careers are those of housewife and mother. Simply to write off these evident and strong desires by most women as "brainwashing" proves far too much; for we can always dismiss any person's values, no matter how deeply held, as the result of "brainwashing." . . .

And so the high rate of conversion claimed by women's liberationists proves nothing either; may not this be the result of "brainwashing" by the female militants? After all, if you are a redhead, and a Redheaded Liberation League suddenly emerges and shouts at you that you are eternally oppressed by vile nonredheads, some of you might well join in the fray—which proves nothing at all about whether or not redheads are *objectively* oppressed.

I do not go so far as the extreme male "sexists" who contend that women *should* confine themselves to home and children and that any search for alternative careers is unnatural. On the other hand, I do not see much more support for the opposite contention that domestic-type women are violating *their* natures. There is in this, as in all matters, a division of labor; and in a free-market society, every individual will enter those fields and areas of work which he or she finds most attractive. The proportion of working women is far higher than even twenty years ago, and that is fine; but it is still a minority of females, and that's fine too. Who are you or I to tell anyone, male or female, what occupation he or she should enter?

Furthermore, the women's libs have fallen into a logical trap in their charge of centuries of male brainwashing. For if this charge be true, then *why have* men been running the culture over eons of time? Surely, this cannot be an accident. Isn't this evidence of male superiority?

> It is *men*, not women, who are more likely to be the oppressed class, or gender, in our society.

The Friedanites, who call stridently for equality of income and position, have, however, been outpaced in recent months by the more militant women's liberationists, or "new feminists," women who work with the older movement but consider them conservative "Aunt Toms." These new militants, who have been getting most of the publicity, persistently liken their alleged oppression to that of blacks and, like the black movement, reject equality and integration for a radical change in society. They call for the revolutionary abolition of alleged male rule and its supposed corollary, the family. Displaying a deepseated and scarcely concealed hatred of men *per se*, these females call for all-women communes, State-run children, test-tube babies, or just simply the "cutting up of men," as the real founder of militant women's lib, Valerie Solanis, put it in her SCUM (Society for Cutting Up Men) Manifesto. . . .

Men, Not Women, Are Oppressed

I believe that modern American marriages are, by and large, conducted on a basis of equality, but I also believe that the opposite contention is far closer to the truth than that of the New Feminists: namely, that it is *men*, not women, who are more likely to be the oppressed class, or gender, in our society, and that it is far more the men who are the "blacks," the slaves, and women their masters. In the first place, the female militants claim that marriage is a diabolical institution by which husbands enslave their wives and force them to rear children and do housework. But let us consider: in the great majority of the cases, *who* is it that insists on marriage, the man or the woman? Everyone knows the answer. And if this great desire for marriage is the result of male brainwashing, as the women's libs contend, then how is it that so many men resist marriage, resist this prospect of their lifelong seat upon the throne of domestic "tyranny"?

Indeed, as capitalism has immensely lightened the burden of housework through improved technology,

In the late 1960s and early 1970s, critics argued that improvements in technology gave wives plenty of free time to pursue leisure activities such as group painting classes. **(Ralph Crane/Time & Life Pictures/Getty Images.)**

many wives have increasingly constituted a kept leisure class. In the middle-class neighborhood in which I live, I see them, these "oppressed" and hard-faced viragoes, strutting down the street in their mink stoles to the next bridge or mah-jongg game, while their husbands are working themselves into an early coronary down in the garment district to support their helpmeets. . . .

> Too many American men live in a matriarchy, dominated first by Momism, then by female teachers, and then by their wives.

The women's libs claim that men are the masters because they are doing most of the world's work. But, if we look back at the society of the slave South, who indeed did the work? It is always the slaves who do the work, while the masters live in relative idleness off the fruits of their labor. To the extent that husbands work and support the family, while wives enjoy a kept status, who then are the masters?

There is nothing new in this argument, but it is a point that has been forgotten amidst the current furor. It has been noted for years—and especially by Europeans and Asians—that too many American men live in a matriarchy, dominated first by Momism, then by female teachers, and then by their wives. . . .

And as for men forcing women to bear and rear children, *who*, again, in the vast majority of cases, is the party in the marriage most eager to have children? Again, everyone knows the answer. . . .

Marriage Helps Women

The ultimate test of whether women are enslaved or not in the modern marriage is the one of "natural law": to consider what would happen if indeed the women's libs had their way and there were no marriage. In that situation, and in a consequently promiscuous world, what would happen to the children? The answer is that the only visible and demonstrable parent would be the mother.

Only the mother would have the child, and therefore *only the mother* would be stuck with the child. In short, the women militants who complain that they are stuck with the task of raising the children should heed the fact that, in a world without marriage, they would *also* be stuck with the task of earning all of the income for their children's support. I suggest that they contemplate this prospect long and hard before they continue to clamor for the abolition of marriage and the family. . . .

The more radical feminists are not content with such a piddling solution as day-care centers (besides who but *women*, other women this time, would be staffing these centers?). What they want, as Susan Brownmiller indicates in her *New York Sunday Times Magazine* article (March 15, 1970), is total husband-wife equality in all things, which means equally shared careers, equally shared housework, and equally shared child rearing. Brownmiller recognizes that this would have to mean *either* that the husband works for six months and the wife for the next six months, with each alternating six months of child rearing, or that each work half of every day and so alternate the child rearing each halfday. Whichever path is chosen, it is all too clear that this total equality could only be pursued if both parties are willing to live permanently on a hippie, subsistence, part-time-job level. For what career of any importance or quality can be pursued in such a fleeting and haphazard manner? Above the hippie level, then, this alleged "solution" is simply absurd. . . .

An Attack on Sex

At the hard inner core of the Women's Liberation Movement lies a bitter, extremely neurotic if not psychotic, man-hating lesbianism. The quintessence of the New Feminism is revealed.

Is this spirit confined to a few extremists? Is it unfair to tar the whole movement with the brush of the Lesbian

Rampant? I'm afraid not. For example, one motif now permeating the entire movement is a strident opposition to men treating women as "sex objects." This supposedly demeaning, debasing, and exploitative treatment extends from pornography to beauty contests, to advertisements of pretty models using a product, all the way to wolf whistles and admiring glances at girls in miniskirts. But surely the attack on women as "sex objects" is simply an attack on sex, period, or rather, on hetero-sex. These new monsters of the female gender are out to destroy the lovely and age-old custom—delighted in by normal women the world over—of women dressing to attract men and succeeding at this pleasant task. What a dull and dreary world these termagants would impose upon us! A world where all girls look like unkempt wrestlers, where beauty and attractiveness have been replaced by ugliness and "unisex," where delightful femininity has been abolished on behalf of raucous, aggressive, and masculine feminism.

> Jealousy of pretty and attractive girls does, in fact, lie close to the heart of this ugly movement.

Jealousy of pretty and attractive girls does, in fact, lie close to the heart of this ugly movement. One point that should be noted, for example, in the alleged economic discrimination against women: the fantastic upward mobility, as well as high incomes, available to the strikingly pretty girl. The Women's Libs may claim that models are exploited, but if we consider the enormous pay that the models enjoy—as well as their access to the glamorous life—and compare it with their opportunity cost foregone in other occupations such as waitress or typist—the charge of exploitation is laughable indeed. . . .

Woman as "sex objects"? Of course they are sex objects and, praise the Lord, they always will be. (Just as men, of course, are sex objects to women.) As for the wolf whistles, it is impossible for any meaningful relationship to be established on the street or by looking at ads, and so in these roles women properly remain solely as sex objects. When deeper relationships are established between men and women, they each become *more* than sex objects to each other; they each hopefully become love objects as well. It would seem banal even to bother mentioning this, but in today's increasingly degenerate intellectual climate no simple truths can any longer be taken for granted.

Contrast to the strident women's liberationists the charming letter in the *New York Sunday Times* (March 29, 1970) by Susan L. Peck. . . . After decrying the female maladjustment exhibited in the "liberation movement," Mrs. Peck concludes: "I, for one, adore men and I'd rather see than be one!" Hooray, and hopefully Mrs. Peck speaks for the silent majority of American womanhood.

Liberation Is of Benefit to Women, Although Some Doubt the Need for It

Black Maria

The following article from a women's literary magazine answers questions women are asking about the liberation movement. Some feel that a movement is not needed because an individual who wants liberation can get it; however, the article says, calls for changes in social custom are not effective unless made by large numbers of people. Among the magazine's contentions: A liberated woman does not depend on custom, but is concerned with fulfilling her own potential; women gain strength through sisterhood with other women; it is not true that working women neglect their children—they are able to be better mothers than they would be as frustrated and lonely housewives; and it is all right for a woman to want to be pretty as long as she is not purposely trying to attract a man.

SOURCE. "Why Women's Liberation?," *Black Maria*, 1971. Copyright © 1971 by The Chicago Women's Liberation Union. All rights reserved. Reproduced by permission.

Over the last year we have heard many women express their opinions and doubts on the subject of women's liberation. These are some of the issues raised in rap groups, at speaking engagements, and overheard conversations among women. In our own group we have often struggled to find some of the answers. It's presumptuous to say the following are complete answers or that every woman would answer them in this way (in fact we were not able to come to a consensus on each question in our own group). Our hope is that the following discussions will provide a starting place for deeper thought.

Why do you need a movement? If you really want liberation you can get it.

The society has established standards which prevent individuals from fulfilling their potentials (i.e. a woman should get married and take care of children). A movement helps change the climate of social custom in order that women have the freedom to choose alternatives to the previously rigid customs. Only when large numbers of people demand a change to their oppression are they taken seriously, and after a while demands that seemed silly at first become thought of as perfectly acceptable; to reach this level of tolerance, women must discover their potential and begin to react against the forces obstructing them from their goals.

What does a liberated woman have that an unliberated woman doesn't have?

A sense of her own identity and the realization that her life is her own to control. She is not dependent on other people for her security—emotional and monetary—nor does she believe what social custom has determined is her nature. She rejects the idea of women's natural dependency and passivity as a myth, and is concerned with the fulfillment of her potential as a person.

I don't like women. I get along better with men.

This is one of the most common statements by women about women. And it is one of the first emotions to be totally transformed as a woman begins to question what society and men expect of her. Rap groups, small gatherings where women meet to talk about their lives and feelings, often help us to understand how much we really have in common, what and who all of us are up against. In the long run, we have realized there is nowhere to turn but to each other. Hundreds, thousands of women are finding strength, a real feeling of sisterhood by uniting with other women. We are rediscovering ourselves.

Equal Rights Are Due to All Human Beings

Doesn't women's liberation discriminate against men (or . . . aren't you being unfair—more strongly stated— aren't you a man hater)?

It seems when the issues of equal jobs and equal pay are discussed this issue is raised. Women are not asking for "token" jobs and pay which another person is better qualified to receive. They are struggling to inch their way into those skills, professions and academic endeavors which they have the aptitude, strength and interest to succeed in. Women are not saying these are rights due only to them but human rights belonging to all. They have a history of struggling against discrimination, not of promoting it.

> Women are not saying these are rights due only to them but human rights belonging to all.

Aside from the struggle for a decent job and pay commensurate to the work exchanged women are often

Radical Feminists' Controversial View of Family Life

In flagrant disregard for the ethos of the sixties, we advocated celibacy as the appropriate alternative to abusive relationships and considerably downplayed the importance of sex. We thought that the ideology of sex as a *need* was a myth perpetrated by men for their own convenience. We took for granted and, indeed, would have insisted on our own sexual freedom. But we classed sex with other enjoyable but optional activities: fun at the beach, ice cream sundaes, amusement park rides. We might choose to do any of these occasionally, but we would consider the price that was paid. If the price was too high, any could be passed up without regret.

Beyond the matter of whether one ought to stay in an abusive relationship, we questioned how much time and energy ought to go into working out "personal" relationships even of a more promising sort, and asked whether women ought to be devoting themselves to raising children. Although we didn't condemn good sexual relationships or worthwhile family life, should these be found, it is true that, at that historical moment, we thought it best for women to stay free for making the revolution. Even good relationships take time and energy, time and energy that we needed

forced (emotionally and physically) to perform an additional multitude of chores and responsibilities; supervising children, washing clothes and dishes, cooking.... All this takes place after a work day which is as grinding and tiring as any males. This not only exhausts her but tends to shackle her time, keeping her from more stimulating endeavors.

Do mothers in the Women's Liberation Movement neglect their children?

I think that women who are working for equality and who are finding their own lives freer can give more to their children. Many women who are feeling the frustrations and loneliness of being a housewife take it out on in getting the word to women about the possibility of a better way of life, time and energy that we needed for the struggle. And isn't it obvious that a *guerrilla* [one who engages in action against the established order] must be free? Hence we wondered at women who professed to be dedicated to fighting for female liberation and who also chose to have children. We felt that children became the hostages of the system; women's need to protect children makes us vulnerable to male threats and bribes. We might be willing to bring the world down on our own heads through a revolution total enough to effect true liberation for all, but we flinch in contemplating the danger to innocent little ones. Of course, in our apocalyptic thinking, we never envisaged this struggle being one that would go on for twenty, fifty, a hundred years. In this, too, we were progeny of the sixties: we were going to remake the world in the next two or three or five years. There would be plenty of time for "a personal life" later.

SOURCE. *Dana Densmore, "A Year of Living Dangerously: 1968," in* The Feminist Memoir Project, *Rachel DuPlessis and Anne Snitow, eds. New York: Three Rivers Press, 1998, pp. 86–87.*

the children by being bitchy and overly demanding. It is also a freeing thing for children who now have a mother who can really relate to them, instead of one who is caught up in the game playing that goes on in so many families.

Does wanting to be pretty mean you're a cop-out?

No. A movement should make it possible for women to find support for working towards the realization of important goals, it should not restrict or dictate "correct" ways of dressing or acting or thinking. There is room among people who agree on some points to be different: ways of dressing are not intrinsic to the question of women's freedom as concerns her inner needs.

In 1971, Linda Stancil of Charlotte, North Carolina, struggles with household chores, caring for her children, and a full-time job four years after separating from her husband. Many argue that traditional "women's work" is just as important as any "man's job." (**AP Photo.**)

The reaction against a "pretty" looking woman assumes that she is looking that way for the purpose of attracting someone to her, whereas she may only be living up to her own standards of being comfortable.

Don't most women who join women's liberation do so because they're ugly?

The women's movement encourages us to take off our masks, to look honestly at our lives, to take risks, to speak freely about our needs and desires, to offer friendship, affection, and understanding to other women, to struggle for the right of all women, all people, to choose what they will become. Ugliness is not physical—it is anything social, political, or psychological which limits or denies full human development (beauty).

Congress Must Enact an Equal Rights Amendment to the US Constitution

Shirley Chisholm

In the following speech to the US House of Representatives, a congresswoman discusses the prejudice against college-educated women when they seek jobs in fields other than those traditionally considered appropriate for them. She herself has encountered more discrimination because she is a woman than because she is black, she says. Prejudice against blacks is becoming unacceptable to Americans even though it still exists, but bias against women is accepted. While laws will not change this attitude, they can at least cause people to examine it. In her opinion existing laws do not adequately protect women's rights. On the other hand, the laws designed to give women special protection at work, which opponents of an equal rights amendment fear it would eliminate, she says are not needed because working people of both sexes

SOURCE. Shirley Chisholm, "Speech in the House of Representatives," May 21, 1969.

should be protected. Shirley Chisholm was a representative from New York. In 1971 she became the first woman and first African American to run for president of the United States.

M r. Speaker, when a young woman graduates from college and starts looking for a job, she is likely to have a frustrating and even demeaning experience ahead of her. If she walks into an office for an interview, the first question she will be asked is, "Do you type?"

There is a calculated system of prejudice that lies unspoken behind that question. Why is it acceptable for women to be secretaries, librarians, and teachers, but totally unacceptable for them to be managers, administrators, doctors, lawyers, and Members of Congress?

The unspoken assumption is that women are different. They do not have executive ability orderly minds, stability, leadership skills, and they are too emotional.

It has been observed before that society for a long time discriminated against another minority, the blacks, on the same basis—that they were different and inferior. The happy little homemaker and the contented "old darkey" on the plantation were both produced by prejudice.

> In the political world I have been far oftener discriminated against because I am a woman than because I am black.

As a black person, I am no stranger to race prejudice. But the truth is that in the political world I have been far oftener discriminated against because I am a woman than because I am black.

Prejudice against blacks is becoming unacceptable although it will take years to eliminate it. But it is doomed because, slowly, white America is beginning to admit that it exists. Prejudice against women is still acceptable. There is very little understanding yet of the immorality

The Equal Rights Amendment to the US Constitution

Section 1. Equality of rights under the law shall not be denied or abridged by the United States or by any State on account of sex.

Section 2. The Congress shall have the power to enforce, by appropriate legislation, the provisions of this article.

Section 3. This amendment shall take effect two years after the date of ratification.

This amendment was presented to the states for ratification by Congress on March 22, 1972. It failed to be ratified by the required number of states and expired on June 30, 1982.

involved in double pay scales and the classification of most of the better jobs as "for men only."

More than half of the population of the United States is female. But women occupy only 2 percent of the managerial positions. They have not even reached the level of tokenism yet. No women sit on the AFL-CIO council or Supreme Court. There have been only two women who have held Cabinet rank, and at present there are none. Only two women now hold ambassadorial rank in the diplomatic corps. In Congress, we are down to one Senator and 10 Representatives.

Considering that there are about 3 1/2 million more women in the United States than men, this situation is outrageous.

It is true that part of the problem has been that women have not been aggressive in demanding their rights. This was also true of the black population for

Congresswoman Shirley Chisholm, seen here in 1969, said that she had encountered more discrimination for being a woman than for being black. **(AP Photo/ Charles Gorry.)**

many years. They submitted to oppression and even co-operated with it. Women have done the same thing. But now there is an awareness of this situation particularly among the younger segment of the population.

As in the field of equal rights for blacks, Spanish-Americans, the Indians, and other groups, laws will not change such deep-seated problems overnight. But they can be used to provide protection for those who are most abused, and to begin the process of evolutionary change by compelling the insensitive majority to reexamine its unconscious attitudes.

Reintroducing the Equal Rights Amendment

It is for this reason that I wish to introduce today a proposal that has been before every Congress for the last 40 years and that sooner or later must become part of the basic law of the land—the equal rights amendment.

Let me note and try to refute two of the commonest arguments that are offered against this amendment. One is that women are already protected under the law and do not need legislation. Existing laws are not adequate to secure equal rights for women. Sufficient proof of this is the concentration of women in lower paying, menial, unrewarding jobs and their incredible scarcity in the upper level jobs. If women are already equal, why is it such an event whenever one happens to be elected to Congress?

It is obvious that discrimination exists. Women do not have the opportunities that men do. And women that do not conform to the system, who try to break with the accepted patterns, are stigmatized as "odd" and "unfeminine." The fact is that a woman who aspires to be chairman of the board, or a Member of the House, does so for exactly the same reasons as any man. Basically, these are that she thinks she can do the job and she wants to try.

A second argument often heard against the equal rights amendment is that is would eliminate legislation that many States and the Federal Government have enacted giving special protection to women and that it would throw the marriage and divorce laws into chaos.

As for the marriage laws, they are due for a sweeping reform, and an excellent beginning would be to wipe the existing ones off the books. Regarding special protection for working women, I cannot understand why it should be needed. Women need no protection that men do not need. What we need are laws to protect working people, to guarantee them fair pay, safe working conditions, protection against sickness and layoffs, and provision for dignified, comfortable retirement. Men and women need these things equally. That one sex needs protection more than the other is a male supremacist myth as ridiculous and unworthy of respect as the white supremacist myths that society is trying to cure itself of at this time.

Injustice to Women Is the Result of Outdated Myths

Gloria Steinem

In the following testimony during US Senate hearings on the Equal Rights Amendment in 1970, a prominent feminist figure tells why she believes such an amendment is needed. She has personally experienced discrimination because of her sex—she has been refused service in restaurants and been rejected for apartment rentals and membership in groups. Yet, she says, most women have encountered even more discrimination than she has. She argues that this is result of the myths that women are biologically inferior to men; that they are already treated equally; that they are well enough off economically; that children need full-time mothers; and that the women's movement cannot gain serious political power. Gloria Steinem is a well-known writer, lecturer, editor, and activist. She cofounded *Ms.* magazine and has authored several books.

SOURCE. Gloria Steinem, "Testimony Before Senate Hearings on Equal Rights Amendment," May 6, 1970.

My name is Gloria Steinem. I am a writer and editor. I have worked in several political campaigns, and am currently a member of the Policy Council of the Democratic National Committee.

During twelve years of working for a living, I've experienced much of the legal and social discrimination reserved for women in this country. I have been refused service in public restaurants, ordered out of public gathering places, and turned away from apartment rentals, all for the clearly-stated, sole reason that I am a woman.

Women demonstrated inside Tom Brown's Bar, a male-only establishment in New York City, on August 26, 1971. (**AP Photo/ Anthony Camerano.**)

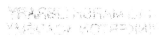

And all without the legal remedies available to blacks and other minorities. I have been excluded from professional groups, writing assignments on so-called "unfeminine" subjects such as politics, full participation in the Democratic Party, jury duty, and even from such small male privileges as discounts on airline fares. Most important to me, I have been denied a society in which women are encouraged, or even allowed, to think of themselves as first-class citizens and responsible human beings.

However, after two years of researching the status of American women, I have discovered that I am very, very lucky. Most women, both wage-earners and housewives, routinely suffer more humiliation and injustice than I do.

As a freelance writer, I don't work in the male-dominated hierarchy of an office. (Women, like blacks and other visibly-different minorities, do better in individual professions such as the arts, sports, or domestic work; anything in which they don't have authority over white males.) I am not one of the millions of women who must support a family. Therefore, I haven't had to go on welfare because there are no day care centers for my children while I work, and I haven't had to submit to the humiliating welfare inquiries about my private and sexual life, inquiries from which men are exempt. I haven't had to brave the sex bias of labor unions and employers, only to see my family subsist on a median salary 40% less than the male median salary.

I hope this committee will hear the personal, daily injustices suffered by many women—professionals and day laborers, women house-bound by welfare as well as suburbia. We have all been silent for too long. We won't be silent anymore.

The truth is that all our problems stem from the same sex-based myths. We may appear before you as white radicals or the middle-aged middleclass or black soul sisters, but we are *all* sisters in fighting against these outdated myths. Like racial myths, they have been reflected in our laws. Let me list a few:

Myth: Women Are Biologically Inferior to Men

In fact, an equally good case can be made for the reverse. Women live longer than men, even when the men are not subject to business pressures. Women survived Nazi concentration camps better, keep cooler heads in emergencies currently studied by disaster-researchers, are protected against heart attacks by their female sex hormones, and are so much more durable at every stage of life that nature must conceive 20 to 50 percent more males in order to keep some balance going.

Man's hunting activities are forever being pointed to as tribal proof of superiority. But while he was hunting, women built houses, tilled the fields, developed animal husbandry, and perfected language.

Men, being all alone in the bush, often developed into a creature as strong as women, fleeter of foot, but not very bright.

> The difference *between* two races or two sexes is much smaller than the differences to be found *within* each group.

However, I don't want to prove the superiority of one sex to another. That would only be repeating a male mistake. English scientists once definitively proved, after all, that the English were descended from the angels, while the Irish were descended from the apes: it was the rationale for England's domination of Ireland for more than a century. The point is that science is used to support current myth and economics almost as much as the church was.

What we do know is that the difference *between* two races or two sexes is much smaller than the differences to be found *within* each group. Therefore, in spite of the slide show on female inferiorities that I understand was shown to you yesterday, the law makes much more sense when it treats individuals, not groups bundled together by some condition of birth.

A word should be said about Dr. [Sigmund] Freud, the great 19th century perpetuator of female inferiority. Many of the differences he assumed to be biological, and therefore changeless, have turned out to be societal, and have already changed. Penis Envy, for instance, is clinically disappearing. Just as black people envied white skins, 19th century women envied penises. A second-class group envies whatever it is that makes another group first class.

Myth: Women Are Already Treated Equally in This Society

I'm sure there has been ample testimony to prove that equal pay for equal work, equal chance for advancement, and equal training or encouragement is obscenely scarce in every field, even those—like food and fashion industries—that are supposedly "feminine."

A deeper result of social and legal injustice, however, is what sociologists refer to as "Internalized Aggression." Victims of aggression absorb the myth of their own inferiority, and come to believe that their group is in fact secondclass.

> Women suffer . . . secondclass treatment from the moment they are born.

Women suffer this secondclass treatment from the moment they are born. They are expected to *be* rather than achieve, to function biologically rather than learn. A brother, whatever his intellect, is more likely to get the family's encouragement and education money, while girls are often pressured to conceal ambition and intelligence, to "Uncle Tom."

I interviewed a New York public school teacher who told me about a black teenager's desire to be a doctor.

With all the barriers in mind, she suggested he be a veterinarian instead.

The same day, a high school teacher mentioned a girl who wanted to be a doctor. The teacher said, "How about a nurse—"

Teachers, parents, and the Supreme Court may exude a protective, well-meaning rationale, but limiting the individual's ambition is doing no one a favor. Certainly not this country. It needs all the talent it can get.

Myth: American Women Hold Great Economic Power

51% of all shareholders in this country are women. That's a favorite male-chauvinist statistic. However, the number of shares they hold is so small that the total is only 18% of all shares. Even those holdings are often controlled by men.

Similarly, only 5% of all the people in the country who receive $10,000 a year or more, earned or otherwise, are women. And that includes all the famous rich widows.

The constantly-repeated myth of our economic power seems less testimony to our real power than to the resentment of what little power we do have.

Myth: Children Must Have Full-Time Mothers

American mothers spend more time with their homes and children than those of any other society we know about. In the past, joint families, servants, a prevalent system in which grandparents [raised] the children, or family field work in the agrarian systems—all these factors contributed more to child care than the labor-saving devices of which we are so proud.

The truth is that most American children seem to be suffering from too much Mother, and too little Father. Part of the program of Women's Liberation is a return of fathers to their children. If laws permit women equal

> When women dare to leave [their 19th century roles], they are ridiculed.

work and pay opportunities, men will then be relieved of their role as sole breadwinner. Fewer ulcers, fewer hours of meaningless work, equal responsibility for his own children: these are a few of the reasons that Women's Liberation is Men's Liberation, too.

As for the psychic health of the children, studies show that the quality of time spent by parents is more important than the quantity. The most damaged children were not those whose mothers worked, but those whose mothers preferred to work but stayed home out of role-playing desire to be a "good mother."

Myth: The Women's Movement Is Not Political, Won't Last, or Is Somehow Not "Serious"

When black people leave their 19th century roles, they are feared. When women dare to leave theirs, they are ridiculed. We understand this, and accept the burden of ridicule. It won't keep us quiet anymore.

Similarly, it shouldn't deceive male observers into thinking this is somehow a joke. We are 51% of the population, we are essentially united on these issues across boundaries of class or race or age, and we may well end by changing this society more than the civil rights movement. That is an apt parallel. We, too, have our right wing and left wing, our separatists, gradualists, and Uncle Toms. But we are changing our own consciousness, and that of the country. [Friedrich] Engels noted the relationship of the authoritarian, nuclear family to capitalism: the father as capitalist, the mother as means of production, and the children as labor. He said the family would change as the economic system did, and that seems to have happened, whether we want to admit it or not. Women's bodies will no longer be owned by the state for the production of workers and soldiers: birth control and abortion are facts of everyday life. The new family is an egalitarian family.

[Swedish sociologist] Gunnar Myrdal noted thirty years ago the parallel between women and Negroes in this country. Both suffered from such restricting social myths as: smaller brains, passive natures, inability to govern themselves (and certainly not white men), sex objects only, childlike natures, special skills and the like. When evaluating a general statement about women, it might be valuable to substitute "black people" for "women"—just to test the prejudice at work.

And it might be valuable to do this Constitutionally as well. Neither group is going to be content as a cheap labor pool anymore. And neither is going to be content without full Constitutional rights.

Finally, I would like to say one thing about this time in which I am testifying.

I had deep misgivings about discussing this topic when National Guardsmen are occupying our campuses, the country is being turned against itself in a terrible polarization, and America is enlarging an already inhuman and unjustifiable war. But it seems to me that much of the trouble this country is in has to do with the Masculine Mystique; with the myth that masculinity somehow depends on the subjugation of other people. It is a bi-partisan problem: both our past and current Presidents seem to be victims of this myth, and to behave accordingly.

Women are not more moral than men. We are only uncorrupted by power. But we do not want to imitate men, to join this country as it is, and I think our very participation will change it. Perhaps women elected leaders—and there will be many more of them—will not be so likely to dominate black people or yellow people or men; anybody who looks different from us.

After all, we won't have our masculinity to prove.

The ERA Would Eliminate Women's Existing Privileges

Phyllis Schlafly

The following article is famous as the one that started the campaign to defeat the Equal Rights Amendment. In it, the woman who led that campaign argues that American women are highly privileged and the ERA would mean giving up those privileges. The traditional family is advantageous for women, she says, because they can enjoy the achievement of having children while men support them, and thanks to modern technology they do not have to do the hard work required of homemakers in former times and in many other countries. Also, wives have a legal share in their husbands' property that they would lose if protective laws were repealed for the sake of equal rights. In her opinion, it would be foolish for women to "lower themselves" by demanding equality. Phyllis Schlafly, a lawyer, is the founder and president of the Eagle

SOURCE. Phyllis Schlafly, "What's Wrong with Equal Rights for Women?" *Feminist Fantasies*. Dallas: Spence Publishing, 2003, pp. 89–93. Copyright © 2003 by Phyllis Schlafly. All rights reserved. Reproduced by permission.

Forum, a conservative volunteer political organization. She writes a regular newsletter and a syndicated column, hosts a syndicated radio show, and is the author of many books.

Of all the classes of people who ever lived, the American woman is the most privileged. We have the most rights and rewards, and the fewest duties. Our unique status is the result of a fortunate combination of circumstances.

We have the immense good fortune to live in a civilization that respects the family as the basic unit of society. This respect is part and parcel of our laws and customs. It is based on the fact of life—which no legislation or agitation can erase—that women have babies and men don't.

If you don't like this fundamental difference, you will have to take up your complaint with God because He created us this way. The fact that women, not men, have babies is not the fault of selfish and domineering men, or the establishment, or any clique of conspirators who want to oppress women. It's simply the way God made us.

> The fact that women, not men, have babies is not the fault of . . . any clique of conspirators who want to oppress women.

Traditional Families Are Advantageous to Women

Our Judeo-Christian civilization has developed the law and custom that, since women bear the physical consequences of the sex act, men must be required to pay in other ways. These laws and customs decree that a man must carry his share by physical protection and financial support of his children and of the woman who bears his children, and also by a code of behavior that benefits and protects both the woman and the children.

Phyllis Schlafly (left) opposed the passage of the Equal Rights Amendment, which she believed would be bad for women. (Bill Pierce/ Time & Life Pictures/ Getty Images.)

This is accomplished by the institution of the family. Our respect for the family as the basic unit of society, which is ingrained in the laws and customs of our Judeo-Christian civilization, is the greatest single achievement in the history of women's rights. It assures a woman the most precious and important right of all—the right to keep her own baby and to be supported and protected in the enjoyment of watching her baby grow and develop.

The institution of the family is advantageous for women for many reasons. After all, what do we want out of life? To love and be loved? Mankind has not discovered a better nest for a lifetime of reciprocal love. A sense of achievement? A man may search thirty to forty years for accomplishment in his profession. A woman can enjoy real achievement when she is young by having a baby. She can have the satisfaction of doing a job well—and being recognized for it.

Do we want financial security? We are fortunate to have the great legacy of Moses, the Ten Commandments, especially "Honor thy father and thy mother that thy days may be long upon the land." Children are a woman's best social security—her best guarantee of social benefits such as old age pension, unemployment compensation, worker's compensation, and sick leave. The family gives a woman the physical, financial, and emotional security of the home for all her life.

American Women Are Better Off than Those in Other Countries

The second reason why American women are a privileged group is that we are the beneficiaries of a tradition of special respect for women that dates from the Christian Age of Chivalry. The honor and respect paid to Mary, the Mother of Christ, resulted in all women, in effect, being put on a pedestal.

This respect for women is not just the lip service that politicians pay to God, Motherhood, and the Flag. It is not—as some agitators seem to think—just a matter of opening doors for women, seeing that they are seated first, carrying their bundles, and helping them in and out of automobiles. Such good manners are merely the superficial evidences of a total attitude toward women that expresses itself in many more tangible ways, such as money.

In other civilizations, such as the African and the American Indian, the men strut around wearing feathers and beads, and hunting and fishing (great sport for men!), while the women do all the hard, tiresome drudgery, including the tilling of the soil (if any is done), the hewing of wood, the making of fires, the carrying of water, as well as the cooking, sewing, and caring for babies.

This is not the American way because we were lucky enough to inherit the traditions of the Age of Chivalry.

In America, a man's first significant purchase (after a car) is a diamond for his bride, and the largest financial investment of his life is a home for her to live in. American husbands work hours of overtime to keep their wives in fashion, and to pay premiums on their life insurance policies to provide for their widow's comfort (benefits in which the husband can never share).

In the states that follow the English common law, a wife has a dower right in her husband's real estate which he cannot take away from her during life or by his will. A man cannot dispose of his real estate without his wife's signature. Any sale is subject to her one-third interest.

Women fare even better in the states that follow the Spanish and French community property laws, such as California, Arizona, Texas, and Louisiana. The philosophy of the Spanish and French law is that a wife's work in the home is just as valuable as a husband's work at his job. In community-property states, a wife owns one-half of all the property and income her husband earns during the marriage, and he cannot take it away from her.

In Illinois, as a result of agitation by "equal rights" fanatics, the real-estate dower laws were repealed as of January 1, 1972. This means that in Illinois a husband can now sell the family home, spend the money on his girlfriend or gamble it away, and his faithful wife of thirty years cannot stop him. "Equal rights" fanatics have also deprived women in Illinois and in some other states of most of their basic common-law rights to recover damages for breach of promise to marry, seduction, criminal conversation, and alienation of affections.

Technological Innovation Has Liberated Women from Drudgery

The third reason why American women are so well off is that the American free enterprise system has produced remarkable inventors who have lifted the backbreaking "women's work" from our shoulders.

In other countries and in other eras, it was truly said that "Man may work from sun up to sun down, but woman's work is never done." Women labored every waking hour—preparing food on wood-burning stoves, making flour, baking bread in stone ovens, spinning yarn, making clothes, making soap, doing the laundry by hand, heating irons, making candles for light and fires for warmth, and trying to nurse their babies through illnesses without medical care.

The real liberation of women from that drudgery is the American free enterprise system, which stimulated inventive geniuses to pursue their talents—and we all reap the profits. The great heroes of women's liberation are not the straggly haired women on television talk shows and picket lines, but Thomas Edison, who brought the miracle of electricity to our homes to give light and to run all those labor-saving devices—the equivalent, perhaps, of a half-dozen household servants. Or Elias Howe who gave us the sewing machine that resulted in such an abundance of readymade clothing. Or Clarence Birdseye, who invented the process for freezing foods. Or Henry Ford, who mass produced the automobile so it is within the price range of almost every American.

> The claim that American women are downtrodden and unfairly treated is the fraud of the century.

A major occupation of women in other countries is doing their daily shopping for food, which requires carrying their own containers and standing in line at dozens of small shops. They buy only small portions because they can't carry very much and have no refrigerator or freezer to keep a surplus anyway. Our American free enterprise system has given us the gigantic food and packaging industry and beautiful supermarkets, which provide an endless variety of foods, prepackaged for easy carrying and a minimum of waiting. In America, women have freedom from the slavery of standing in line for daily food.

Household duties have been reduced to only a few hours a day, leaving the American woman with plenty of time to moonlight. She can take a full- or part-time paying job, or she can indulge to her heart's content in a tremendous selection of interesting educational or cultural or homemaking or volunteer activities.

It's time to set the record straight. The claim that American women are downtrodden and unfairly treated is the fraud of the century. The truth is that American women never had it so good. Why should we lower ourselves to "equal rights" when we already have the status of special privilege?

Women Throughout the World Have Lower Status than Men

Helvi L. Sipilä

In the following article, a United Nations official reports on the status of women throughout the world in 1975, the thirtieth anniversary of the founding of the UN. Though much has been done toward achieving equal rights, especially through laws, she says, social change has been slow; for example, although women have gained the right to vote and hold office in all member nations, only a small percentage of them do so. The right of women to work has become accepted, but there are a limited number of jobs open to them, and they are paid less than men. In some countries a wife is still legally required to obey her husband, she reports, and everywhere she is expected to take on the entire burden of homemaking. Furthermore, the needs of mothers and children are ignored by the health care policies of many nations. The International Women's Year must focus on eliminating discrimination against

SOURCE. Helvi L. Sipilä, "Women's Lib, 30 Years of Progress," *The UNESCO Courier*, March 1975, pp. 4–9. Copyright © UNESCO 1975. Used by permission of UNESCO.

women, the author writes. Helvi Sipilä, a Finnish lawyer, was the
assistant secretary-general for social development and humanitar-
ian affairs at the United Nations and secretary-general for the UN's
1975 International Women's Year.

Since the U.N. began in 1945 a great deal has been
done to improve the situation and status of women
in the world. Particularly in the legal field, much
has been and is being done to accord women equal rights
with men in political, economic, social and family life.
Age-old traditions, attitudes and practices are still, however, slow to change and the gap between law and reality
still remains very wide.

In the political field, for example, whereas in 1945
women were denied the right to vote in approximately
one third of the U.N.'s 51 Member States, today women
are legally eligible to vote in all elections and to stand
for election on equal terms with men in 124 Member
Nations. Yet, the percentage of women holding policy-
making posts in the local, national and international
areas still remains strikingly small.

In New Zealand, for example, which was the first nation in the world to grant women the vote in 1893, 92 per
cent of the candidates and 95 per cent of those elected in
the last elections (1972) were men. In Egypt, in 1967, 76
per cent of women failed to vote. The highest percent-
ages of political participation in national legislatures are
reported in the U.S.S.R. (35 per cent) and Finland (21.5
per cent).

At the international level, the picture is equally
dismal. In the 28th U.N. General Assembly (1973), for
example, there were only 180 women compared to 2,369
men delegates. There were no women in the delegations
of 55 countries and only one woman in the delegations
of 44 countries.

The Right to Work

In the economic field, considerable progress has been made in the past 25 years. In 1945 women's right to work and to equal conditions of work (including the thorny question of equal pay for work of equal value) was hardly discussed, even in the International Labour Organization [ILO]. Today, these questions are fully accepted as "rights" to be recognized and implemented in practice, albeit progressively and at a very slow pace.

A number of ILO instruments, especially the 1951 Convention on Equal Remuneration for Men and Women Workers for work of equal value and the 1958 Convention on discrimination in employment and occupation, have been landmarks in this process of achieving public acceptance of these rights.

Nevertheless women, who constitute about 562 million workers or 34 per cent of the world's labour force (38 per cent for the developed, 32 per cent for developing countries) are mainly concentrated in a limited number of jobs, frequently at low levels of skills and responsibilities with equally low wages or salaries.

Their work is often not recognized in practice as being of equal value to men's work and their pay for the same job is often lower. And these figures do not take into account the millions of women who are toiling from morning till night as unpaid subsistence farm or domestic workers. There are no statistics to tell us how many women live in such circumstances, nor the extent of their economic output and return.

Statistical data on wage differentials of men and women in the various sectors and occupations are very inadequate, but ILO studies suggest that even in many industrialized countries women's wages are about 50 to 80 per cent of men's for the same work time.

> Some progress has been made through educational measures to eliminate prejudice and discriminatory attitudes based on the stereotyping of sex roles.

The concentration of women in lower ranking positions is found even in the United Nations Secretariat, where approximately 80 per cent of the General Service staff, but only 20 per cent of professional staff, are women. As regards education, while few today would deny women's right to be educated equally with men, women remain in many countries seriously disadvantaged at every level—primary, secondary and at the higher level.

Sex Bias in Education

Particularly in the developed world, some progress has been made through educational measures to eliminate prejudice and discriminatory attitudes based on the stereotyping of sex roles. Changes have included curriculum reform, greater flexibility in the choice of subjects for both boys and girls (both, for example, are now studying the same amount of mathematics, sciences and home economics in some countries) and both are being educated in sex and family life.

Whatever illiteracy prevails, however, the percentage of illiterate females is always higher than that of males. In 1960 the illiteracy rates were 33.5 per cent for men and 44.9 per cent for women. By 1970 these were 28.0 per cent and 40.3 per cent, respectively. In Africa and the Arab States which have the highest rates, the female illiteracy rate dropped from 88.5 to 83.7 per cent and from 90.7 to 85.7 per cent, respectively, in the same decade.

Despite the fact that special efforts have been made in many countries to provide adult literacy classes, a much lower ratio of women than men continue to enroll. This is due mainly to such factors as distance from schools, impracticability of travelling by night, household chores, early marriage, outmoded attitudes and sheer lack of adequate facilities to service the number of illiterate persons.

Photo on following page: Two women show their support of voting rights in 1970. Even though women have gained the right to vote in all UN member nations, only a small percentage do so. (Gabriel Hackett/ Getty Images.)

Access to education of girls and women in different parts of the world also depends on the level of general development of a country. But even in industrialized countries, where primary education is compulsory, differences in curricula, in teaching methods and in subjects available to girls and boys continue to exist. One of the results is the preponderance of women in the labour force in certain fields and their small or complete lack of representation in other fields.

The element of choice may be theoretically present but to a large extent the "choice" is induced by sex-biased education which begins in early childhood. Clearly differential treatment exists equally with regard to vocational training and this leads to different opportunities in employment and occupations, different salaries, wages and occupational hierarchies, no matter what principles of equality exist in law.

> "The principle of equal rights of men and women has now been recognized and written into the basic laws of many countries."

The trend towards the improvement of the legal position of women has accelerated markedly in recent years, and the principle of equal rights of men and women has now been recognized and written into the basic laws of many countries. While, in some instances, formal legal equality has existed since the early part of this century (e.g. Nordic and Eastern European countries), in most cases major changes have taken place only since 1945.

Discrimination Under Civil Law

In the field of civil law, however, and especially family law, the principle of equality has not yet won universal acceptance although there have been noticeable trends in that direction in recent years. Recent or current reforms have done away with legislation which was discriminatory against women and several countries have enacted laws with the aim of achieving a more equitable sharing of rights and responsibilities within the family.

Laws enacted in some countries (e.g. Brazil, France, the Ivory Coast, Luxembourg, Monaco) in the past two decades reveal, for example, discernible trends toward a more even-handed partnership of the spouses in decision-making; towards a more equitable sharing, based on the earning ability of each, of the assets acquired during marriage at the time the marriage is dissolved (e.g. Austria, Canada [various provinces], France, Monaco); towards the recognition of the work of the housewife as a contribution to the assets of the family, assets which should be shared by the spouses (or their heirs) at the dissolution of marriage (e.g. Eastern European countries, and in the United Kingdom [since 1970]).

Some countries, which had not previously done so, adopted legislation recognizing the inheritance rights of the surviving spouse (e.g. France), and equal parental rights and duties, the interest of the child being the paramount consideration. The latter included the granting of full status as a parent to the unmarried mother (e.g. Austria, Sweden).

> The laws of some . . . countries may stipulate that the wife owes obedience to her husband.

The laws of various countries governing divorce have been liberalized to some extent. Divorce is now permitted in countries where previously it was not recognized, e.g. Italy (since 1974), Monaco (since 1970). In Afghanistan (since 1971) the wife now has the legal right to divorce under certain conditions, whereas formerly, it was the exclusive privilege of the husband. In other countries, divorce has been made much easier for both spouses than previously (e.g., Sweden, the United States of America [state of New York]).

In many countries, however, the husband is still recognized in law as the "head of the family" and plays the dominant role in the marriage relationship, the wife being relegated to an inferior position with little or no legal say in decisions affecting herself and other members of the family.

The laws of some of these countries may stipulate that the wife owes obedience to her husband (e.g. Ethiopia, Jordan, Mali, Tunisia). She may need the authorization of her husband or the court to exercise her legal capacity to contract, sue and be sued (e.g. Ecuador, Haiti, Mexico, the Philippines, Uruguay). Her property rights may be limited under the rules governing the property relations of the spouses. Her right to work may be subject to the express or implied authorization of her husband (e.g. Burundi, Ecuador [only to engage in trade or industry], Mali [to engage in trade]). In other countries, however, the law requires that the wife owe obedience to her husband.

Despite the fact that modern legislative trends increasingly recognize the importance of women's employment outside the home, from the viewpoint of overall economic development as well as personal or family need, the role of homemaker is still assigned primarily to the woman, not only through tradition and social custom but also in some instances in law, and she is expected to perform that role without financial compensation during marriage. This may be explicitly formulated in the law or implied in various legal provisions concerning maintenance of the wife and of the family's expenses when these are the main responsibility of the husband.

This problem is of major importance in considering ways to increase opportunities for women to participate in gainful employment and development. Governments and government planners in some countries have begun to realize that functions should be more equitably divided between the sexes so that both may have practical opportunities to participate in parenthood and in employment.

An American Feminist Visits European Women's Groups

In the summer of 1970, I took advantage of a student charter flight to travel in Europe to visit the emerging feminist groups. . . . In Holland I hit pay dirt. Women and younger lefty men had created the "dolleminas." On the other side of the generation gap, Joke Kool-Smit, a professor of languages at the University of Amsterdam, had organized the Dutch equivalent of NOW [National Organization for Women], known as Man/Vrouw/Maatschappij. We hit it off. Sharing experiences and observations with the Dutch women illuminated some of the ways in which both custom and policy controlled women's actions that I had not been able to see up close in my own country. I left lots of American feminist pamphlets with them which Joke later wrote were influential to their thinking. . . .

I only passed through Germany, since I didn't speak German, and spent the next couple of weeks in Denmark, Norway and Sweden, where feminism was flourishing and pretty much everyone my age and younger spoke English. The Danish feminists called themselves Redstockings, after the New York group, but had their own feminist philosophy. The Swedish were very cool and distant. No one would talk to me without a formal introduction and an appointment. I didn't learn a great deal about the Swedish movement beyond the fact that they believed they didn't need one since they were so far ahead of everyone else in the "sex role" debate. In Norway, I found friends . . . [who] asked me to speak at the University of Oslo the week classes started so that local feminists could use the occasion to organize a mass movement. Of course I agreed.

That is why I was in Oslo on August 26, 1970, when American feminists were marching down Fifth Avenue in the first contemporary mass feminist demonstration. I told the Norwegians I needed to do something to commemorate the day and . . . [they said,] "Hold a press conference." . . . I was quite surprised when reporters from the numerous Norwegian papers and the one TV station crowded into a room to hear an obscure American feminist. . . .

My lecture a few days later . . . was a success. . . . Hundreds of people came; many joined. They called themselves Nyfeministene. New groups sprouted everywhere. . . . I've often wondered how their movement fared, though when I read in the papers how many women are running their government, I know they did something right.

SOURCE. Jo Freeman, "On the Origins of the Women's Liberation Movement from a Strictly Personal Perspective," www.jofreeman.com.

It is also being gradually recognized that policies which attempt to give women an equal place with men in economic life, while at the same time confirming women's traditional responsibility for the care of the home and children, have no prospect of fulfilling the first of these aims.

The Needs of Mothers

There is one field in which equality does not arise, but in which the needs and rights of women obviously need protection, and that is maternity. Because of the lack of women's participation in the formulation of policies in the field of health, their special needs for the protection of maternity are often not even known to the decision-makers. This is, therefore, one of the most neglected fields of health care in many countries. Although the availability of health services largely depends on the resources and personnel available, much could be achieved by inexpensive training in health, nutrition and home economics as preventive health services.

In all our efforts to improve the quality of life of all human beings, too little attention is paid to the needs of millions of children and mothers, especially in the developing areas, rural as well as urban. How can we improve the quality of life of a human being born to an illiterate, economically dependent, malnourished, and over-burdened woman, whose health may leave much to be desired and who gives birth to one child per year?

International Women's Year 1975 gives all of us a unique opportunity to focus attention on eliminating these still pervasive discriminations against women, thereby enabling women to more fully participate and contribute to the economic, social and political life of our planet.

The significance of the Year will be what we make of it. It could be a truly historic year—a landmark not only in the history of women's advancement but also in the advancement of humanity as a whole. Let us all work to make it so.

The ERA Alone Will Not End Discrimination Against Women

Betty Ford

The following speech was given by the First Lady at the 1975 International Women's Year conference. She says that, although progress has been made in correcting the problems faced by women, there are still too few opportunities open to them and that the conference should focus on removing the limits imposed on them by social custom. She argues that while the Equal Rights Amendment will help to increase women's options, it is only a beginning, and that supporters must work to counteract the fear of change and confusion that is felt by its opponents. It is unfortunate, she says, that the debate is leading people to underestimate the value of homemaking and motherhood. Those who choose a traditional role should take pride in it; downgrading them is part of the general lack of appreciation of women's talents. Betty Ford, the wife of US president Gerald Ford, was the First Lady of the United States from 1974 to 1977.

SOURCE. Betty Ford, "Remarks to the International Women's Year Conference," ford.utexas.edu, October 25, 1975.

Thank you for inviting me. I am here because I believe the best way to celebrate International Women's Year is to examine the very real problems women face today, not the progress of yesterday.

While many new opportunities are open to women, too many are available only to the lucky few.

Many barriers continue to the paths of most women, even on the most basic issue of equal pay for equal work. And the contributions of women as wives and mothers continue to be underrated.

This year is not the time to cheer the visible few, but to work for the invisible many, whose lives are still restricted by custom and code.

In working sessions of this conference, you will explore many of the formal and informal restrictions that confine women.

Many of these restrictions spring directly from those emotional ideas about what women can do and should do. These definitions of behavior and ability inhibit men and women alike, but the limits on women have been formalized into law and structured into social custom.

For that reason, the first important steps have been to undo the laws that hem women in and lock them out of the mainstream of opportunities.

But my own support of the Equal Rights Amendment has shown what happens when a definition of proper behavior collides with the right of an individual to personal opinions. I do not believe that being First Lady should prevent me from expressing my views.

I spoke out on this important issue because of my deep personal convictions. Why should my husband's job or yours prevent us from being ourselves? Being ladylike does not require silence.

The Equal Rights Amendment when ratified will not be an instant solution to women's problems. It will not alter the fabric of the Constitution or force women away from their families.

It will help knock down those restrictions that have locked women in to old stereotypes of behavior and opportunity. It will help open up more options for women.

The ERA Is Only a Beginning

But it is only a beginning.

The debate over ERA has become too emotional, because of the fears of some—both men and women—about the changes already taking place in America.

> The debate over ERA has become too emotional, because of the fears . . . about the changes already taking place in America.

And part of the job of those of us who support ERA is to help remove this cloud of fear and confusion.

Change by its very nature is threatening, but it is also often productive. And the fight of women to become more productive, accepted human beings is important to all people of either sex and whatever nationality.

I hope 1976 will be the year the remaining four states ratify the 27th amendment. It will be an important symbolic event during our 200th birthday to show that the great American experiment in human freedom continues to expand.

But changing laws, more job opportunities, less financial discrimination and more possibilities for the use of our minds and bodies will only partially change the place of American women.

By themselves they will never be enough, because we must value our own talents before we can expect acceptance from others. The heart of the battle is within.

I have been distressed that one unfortunate outgrowth of the debate has been a lack of appreciation of the role of women as wives and mothers.

In trying to open up new choices and opportunities, women must not underestimate their accomplishments in the home.

Fortunately, I have had the best of two worlds—that of a career woman earning my own living, and that of a homemaker and mother raising four individual and delightful youngsters. I am equally proud of both periods in my life.

Women Must Take Pride in Homemaking

We have to take that "'just" out of "just a housewife" and show our pride in having made the home and family our life's work.

Downgrading this work has been part of the pattern in our society that has undervalued women's talents in all areas.

We have come a long way, but we have a long way to go—part of that distance is within our own mind.

First ladies Betty Ford (left) and Lady Bird Johnson show their support for the Equal Rights Amendment at a rally in October 1981. (Penelope Breese/Liaison/Getty Images.)

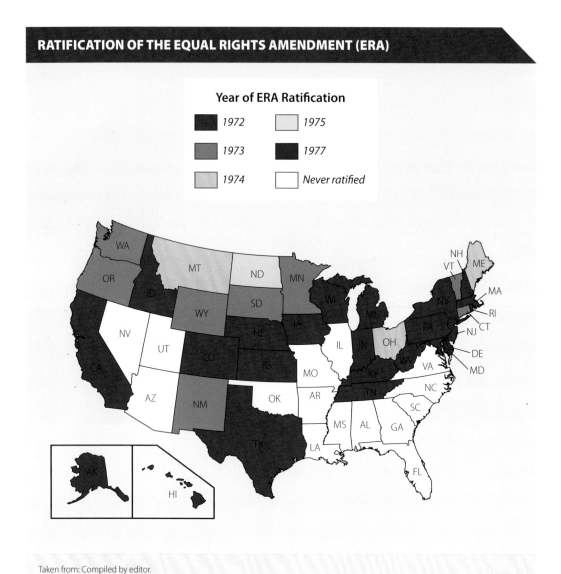

RATIFICATION OF THE EQUAL RIGHTS AMENDMENT (ERA)

Year of ERA Ratification

- 1972
- 1973
- 1974
- 1975
- 1977
- Never ratified

Taken from: Compiled by editor.

ERA will help open some doors. Changing our own attitudes as women will open even more. But legal help and self-help will not be enough.

The long road to equality rests on achievements of women and men in altering how women are treated in every area of everyday life.

That is why this conference is so important, because you are looking at the patterns of discrimination which must be ended before women are truly free.

> The search for human freedom can never be complete without freedom for women.

Freedom for women to be what they want to be will help complete the circle of freedom America has been striving for during 200 years. As the barriers against freedom for Americans because of race or religion have fallen, the freedom of all has expanded. The search for human freedom can never be complete without freedom for women.

By the end of this century, I hope this nation will be a place where men and women can freely choose their life's work without restrictions or without ridicule.

On the eve of the nation's third century, let us work to end the laws and remove the labels that limit the imagination and the options of men and women alike.

Success will open hearts and minds to new possibilities for all people. Much has been done, much remains, but we must keep moving on.

The Debate Over the ERA Led to Major Changes in the Status of Women

Leslie W. Gladstone

> The following viewpoint explains that both sides in the long and often bitter controversy over the Equal Rights Amendment were highly emotional about it, and the amendment's eventual defeat was both mourned and celebrated. When it was first submitted to the states for ratification in 1972, it appeared likely to become law, but opposition developed quickly. Socially conservative women, shocked by some of its implications, became politically active, the author states. Nevertheless, support for less drastic changes in society's attitude toward women grew, many women's rights measures were passed, and the number of women holding elective office increased. Thus, the effect of the debate on the status of women was positive in the long run, she argues. Leslie W.

SOURCE. Leslie W. Gladstone, "The Long Road to Equality: What Women Won from the ERA Ratification Effort," *Library of Congress: American Memory*. Washington, DC: Library of Congress.

Gladstone is a researcher for the Congressional Record Service of the Library of Congress.

At a National Organization for Women (NOW) rally in Lafayette Park across from the White House, on June 30, 1982, NOW president Eleanor Smeal rallied an estimated two thousand supporters, including seven hundred nurses in town for the American Nurses Association convention. Although they were there that day mourning the defeat of the Equal Rights Amendment (ERA), Smeal urged them not to forget that "We are a majority. We are determined to play majority politics. . . . We are not going to be reduced again to the ladies' auxiliary."

Meanwhile, in San Francisco, outside the Civic Center, about one thousand women counted down the ERA's last six hours, a rain-soaked vigil that was reported, filmed, and recorded by many women journalists and technicians.

That same night, at a party in a Washington, D.C., hotel, the ERA's demise was celebrated by opponents, fourteen hundred strong, as "a great victory for women." The *Washington Post* account of that evening describes the entrance into the ballroom of the leader of the ERA opposition, Phyllis Schlafly, as the band played "Somewhere over the Rainbow." During the festivities, the crowd was entertained with renditions of "Ding, Dong, the Witch Is Dead" and "I Enjoy Being a Girl." Triumphantly addressing the crowd, Schlafly called for "a mighty movement" that will "set America on the right path."

What caused the rejection of the Equal Rights Amendment? Why the intense emotions that caused ERA proponents to write the names of opponents in pigs' blood on the floors of the Illinois state capitol or opponents to pronounce apocalyptically that if the amendment was ratified husbands would no longer have to support their wives, that women would be drafted, and that toilets would be made unisex? What, if any, was the legacy of the often bitter ratification campaign that divided American women for nearly a decade beginning in 1972?

The Origin of the ERA

The proposed Equal Rights Amendment, only fifty-one words in length, was contentious from its inception. In a form suggested by [suffragist] Alice Paul, a constitutional

Many more women hold elective office in the United States following the ERA debates. Former first lady Hillary Rodham Clinton was elected to the Senate in 2000. (Matt Campbell/ AFP/Getty Images.)

amendment was first introduced in 1923—only three years after the Nineteenth Amendment granted women the right to vote—unleashing sixty or more years of national debate. . . .

In the 1960s, the period generally referred to as the second women's rights movement began with John F. Kennedy's appointment of the first President's Commission on the Status of Women (PCSW), chaired by Eleanor Roosevelt. The work of this and other early commissions successfully focused public attention on a broad range of initiatives designed to address the unequal position of American women, both under U.S. law and in customary practice, issues which also found expression in numerous women's rights demonstrations. . . .

"When would the government act?" was the activists' question, and "*Now*" became the mantra. Outraged by the refusal of the newly formed Equal Employment Opportunity Commission to prosecute job discrimination cases on the basis of sex through Title VII of the Civil Rights Act of 1964, Marguerite Rawalt, Betty Friedan, and others founded the National Organization for Women in 1966. Passage of the ERA was its first agenda item. Four years later, on July 20, 1970, Representative Martha Griffiths, a Democrat from Michigan, collected enough signatures for a discharge petition, by-passing veteran House Judiciary Committee chair Emanuel Celler, a liberal Democrat from New York with strong labor ties who had refused to hold hearings on the ERA for two decades. Opening House hearings on the amendment on August 10, Griffiths pleaded, "Give us a chance to show you that those so-called protective laws to aid women— however well intentioned originally—have become in fact restraints, which keep wife, abandoned wife, and widow alike from supporting her family."

Approved by 352-15 in the U.S. House of Representatives in 1971, the amendment moved to the Senate, where Senator Sam Ervin, a Democrat from North

Carolina and chair of the Senate Judiciary Committee, was its chief opponent. A strict constitutionalist, Ervin in fact attacked the amendment on the basis of traditional views of gender. Much anti-ERA literature subsequently was based on Ervin's public statements. Despite continued opposition of some segments of organized labor, the ERA was passed by the Senate on March 22, 1972, and it was submitted to the states for ratification.

The Effort Toward Ratification

In the years between 1972 and 1977, the federal amendment proposing equal rights for women was considered by the legislatures of every state, in some cases more than once, and thirty-five of them ratified it. In addition, between 1971 and 1978, fifteen states adopted equal rights amendments to their own constitutions, providing a legal basis for equal treatment to women in those jurisdictions. These served to demonstrate the protections that such an amendment could provide and as an argument for passage of a federal amendment. At the same time, other states began making changes in their laws to eliminate distinctions that unfairly precluded women from receiving equal treatment.

> One problem encountered early in the ratification campaign was the portrayal of women and women's rights by the press.

One problem encountered early in the ratification campaign was the portrayal of women and women's rights by the press generally, which seemed to enjoy making them subjects of heavy-handed jokes. When Gloria Steinem was invited to speak at a National Press Club luncheon in January 1972, a short time after the club had agreed to admit women journalists, she used the occasion to take up not only the serious issues of feminism and the ERA but also the crippling effect for both sexes of a male-dominated vision of the world. A tape of the session . . . records her comments on the way men tended to assume that they represented the norm, so that when the press presented issues important to the lives of women, reporters seldom found it necessary to seek out women as sources. As an example she cited a recent story on abortion in which the interviewees consisted of a number of men, plus one nun. Conservative women, on the other hand, particularly Schlafly, were convinced that the "liberal" press was on the side of the ERA. . . .

Scholars have speculated about the causes of the dramatic slowing in the ratification process that followed the first three months of 1973. It has been suggested that the Supreme Court's decision on abortion in *Roe v. Wade* on January 22, 1973, coupled with nationwide admiration for Senator Sam Ervin's chairmanship of the Senate Watergate hearings [on the political scandal leading to the resignation of President Richard Nixon] that began in May, made ERA proponents' task much harder. Decriminalization of abortion angered fundamentalists and social conservatives, and Ervin, leader of the Senate opposition to the ERA since 1969 and now seen as a savior of the Constitution, became their champion in the southern states that refused to ratify the ERA.

HOW LANGUAGE HAS CHANGED SINCE THE 1970S

The women's liberation movement succeeded in bringing about lasting changes to everyday terminology. Below are some common words for which gender-neutral replacements have become standard.

policeman	police officer
fireman	firefighter
postman	mail carrier
waiter/waitress	server
chairman	chair
housewife	homemaker
stewardess	flight attendant
salesman (in store)	salesclerk, sales associate
salesman (traveling)	sales representative
workman	worker
repairman	technician
foreman	supervisor
garbageman	trash collector
newsboy	news carrier
watchman	security guard
gunman	shooter
man-made	artificial
man (human race)	humanity
mankind	humankind

Taken from: Compiled by editor.

Preparations for International Women's Year and its culminating event, the National Women's Conference in Houston in 1977, infused the ERA ratification effort with new energy. And just in time, for not only had ratification slowed markedly but five states had voted to rescind their previous ratifications. The designation of 1975 as International Women's Year (IWY), a United Nations initiative, had come in response to the rising demand for women's rights, not only in the United States, but around the world. . . .

Many more socially conservative women were politicized by the Houston conference. Shocked by the delegates' overwhelming support for the ERA, gay rights, federal funding of abortion, government-sponsored child care, and contraception for minors without parental consent, all advocated in the name of "women's rights," they were also angered that this "feminist" convention was supported by taxpayers. A privately funded opposition rally in Houston was held by Schlafly and her Stop ERA and Eagle Forum organizations. The ERA campaign was denounced as an assault on the family and on the role of women as wives and mothers. . . .

> The ERA campaign was denounced as an assault on the family and on the role of women as wives and mothers.

The anti-ERA effort had a strong educational value for conservative women, many of whom became effective lobbyists for their points of view. As the Reverend Jerry Falwell remarked the day after the ERA died, "Phyllis has succeeded in doing something nobody has ever done. . . . She's mobilized the conservative women of this country into a powerful political unit."

At the national level, the case for passage of the amendment was carried to the general public by magazine articles in such publications as *Woman's Day* and *Working Women*. These stories discussed issues like:

- discriminatory wages
- battered wives
- loopholes in a homemaker's right to spousal support
- publicly funded boys-only schools and
- the lack of protections for women in the areas of marital and property rights, child support payments, and credit access. . . .

Although the amendment was ratified by thirty-five states, it did not gain approval of the necessary three-fourths or thirty-eight states before the 1982 deadline.

The Lasting Impact of the Debate

There is no question, however, that public opinion regarding the need for change was substantially altered by the years of debate. Surveys taken by Louis Harris and by the Roper Organization from 1970 through 1985 show steadily growing support for strengthening the status of women. The shift in viewpoints over time are reflected in differing answers to the question, "Do you favor most of the efforts to strengthen and change women's status in society today?" At the beginning of the 1970s, 40 percent of women and 44 percent of men who responded approved the idea. Fifteen years later in 1985, 73 percent of women and 69 percent of men favored such changes.

Out of the gradual shift in public opinion, legislative gains followed, and a significant number of women's rights measures were passed in this period. Between the 92nd Congress, beginning in 1971, and the 95th Congress, ending in 1978, ten statutes were enacted prohibiting discrimination on the basis of sex with regard to education, employment, credit, and housing, more than

> There is no question . . . that public opinion regarding the need for change was substantially altered by the years of debate.

during any other period in the history of the Congress. Other legislation focused on women's interests has been enacted in the years following.

Since the 1980s, with the major civil rights statutes in place, other legislative gains have included measures to:

- provide pension rights and survivor benefits to divorced spouses under various public pension plans
- strengthen the Fair Housing Act to ban discrimination against families with children
- ban discrimination on the basis of sex in public jobs programs
- fund training programs for men and women who are entering nontraditional occupations and for individuals who are single parents or displaced homemakers
- improve child support enforcement programs
- clarify the application of Title IX of the Education Amendments of 1972, which prohibits discrimination on the basis of sex in federally assisted education programs and activities (by restoring the broad coverage originally enacted)
- provide for the protection of jobs and health insurance after childbirth or family health emergencies.

The Supreme Court of the United States also revealed an awareness of the ratification arguments and, in the 1970s and 1980s, moved toward a more rigorous standard of review in sex discrimination cases, although it fell short of applying the "suspect" category test it applied to race and national origin. . . .

Between 1970 and 1990, the number of women winning elective offices increased markedly, and their influence was significant in promoting legislation supportive of women's interests. The number of women mayors in cities with populations over 30,000 increased from 1.6 percent in 1973 to 18 percent in 1993.

In the same period, women in state legislatures grew from 5.6 percent to 20.4 percent, women in the U.S. House of Representatives went from 3.7 percent to 10.8 percent, and women senators from zero to 6 percent.

Other women established "firsts" as candidates. Shirley Chisholm was the first African American woman to run for president in 1972 and Patricia Schroeder ran in 1988. Geraldine Ferraro was nominated by a national party for vice president in 1984.

The importance of electing women to office at all levels is best revealed in the pattern that women office-holders established early on. Many of these women from both parties have tended to promote legislation having an impact on the lives of women, children, and families, in areas such as health, welfare, and education. Many others have supported women's rights generally. Moreover, the influence of elected women has changed over time as their numbers have increased, and they have proved equally effective as men at securing passage of their legislative priorities. . . .

In the end, change over these years came from many quarters and for many reasons. The long public debate over the status of women and the call for a constitutional amendment heightened expectations that changes would be made, and changes did follow.

Women at the grass-roots level joined together in examining problems believed by some to have been caused by gender discrimination and women's less-than-equal status. They reached out for new solutions. Inevitably women on both sides of the ERA question became involved in the political process and began learning how the levers of power are activated at different levels of government. The cumulative effect of all these forces stimulated a chain of elective, legislative, and judicial actions that made, and arguably continue to make, a positive contribution to substantive changes in women's status in this country.

Women's Liberation Advocates Were Active in Britain During the 1970s

Kira Cochrane

In the following article, a British reporter describes women's activism in her country during the 1970s. The first National Women's Liberation Conference there took place in February 1970 and is considered a major landmark in British women's history, she writes. Far more people turned up than had been expected, and there was much excitement then and afterward on the part of women who discovered that they were not alone in their dissatisfaction over the existing inequality between men and women. The excitement died down in the 1980s and division arose between different types of feminists, but in the twenty-first century, she says, it seems that young women are showing new interest in the

---

SOURCE. Kira Cochrane, "Forty Years of Women's Liberation," *The Guardian*, February 26, 2010. Copyright © 2010 by The Guardian. All rights reserved. Reproduced by permission.

movement. Kira Cochrane is a features writer for the *Guardian*, a national daily newspaper in Great Britain.

T he hour was 5.30 A.M.; the date, sometime in the late 1960s; the place, London; and Lois Graessle could be found—as she was many mornings— riding the escalators at stops along the District Line, surreptitiously sticking the message "this ad degrades women" on offensive posters. That was the early shift. Come evening rush hour the stickers and targets would change. Men in suits, umbrella tucked under the arm, briefcase swinging, would suddenly feel the touch of a woman's hand on their back. A sticker was left behind. "This man exploits women."

> " Small groups of women were forming across the country . . . as they realised they weren't alone in their frustrations. "

These were the early days of the second-wave feminist movement in Britain (the first wave was the suffrage campaign). It was a time, says Graessle, of enormous innocence, enthusiasm and creative power, when small groups of women were forming across the country, talking about their circumstances, and feeling the rush of recognition as they realised they weren't alone in their frustrations. Sally Alexander, for instance, was a member of a women's group in Oxford, and says that the talk would focus on "the fact that women were very low paid. That we were expected to become either a nurse or a secretary. That most women were cleaners. Women were the poor. We were picking our way through, exploring the issues." A generation was finding its voice.

The First Women's Liberation Conference in England

That period, in which thousands of feminists experienced the first glimmers of consciousness, reached a

Women train conductors in Great Britain demanded equal status with their male coworkers in 1965. (Manchester Daily Express/SSPL via Getty Images.)

turning point 40 years ago this weekend. This was the occasion of the first ever National Women's Liberation Conference, which took place at Ruskin College, Oxford, between 27 February and 1 March 1970. In the definitive history of the event—Michelene Wandor's collection of interviews, *Once a Feminist*—the historian, Sheila Rowbotham, says that this was the moment from which "a movement could be said to exist." It was therefore one of the biggest landmarks in British women's history.

Not that the planning for the event got off to an auspicious start. Accounts of the story differ, but in the late 1960s, when Rowbotham, then in her 20s, stood up at a gathering for the Ruskin History Workshop—a popular academic conference—and suggested that there should be a meeting about women, she was met with gales of laughter from the predominantly male crowd. Alexander was studying at Ruskin at the time and says that "I remember sitting on a table, and thinking, 'How odd.' I joined in the smiles, but then walked off and thought, 'Why did they laugh?' We talked about it, and Sheila said: 'Well, women just aren't taken seriously.'"

Planning began in earnest for what was initially to be a straightforward female history conference. Then, says Rowbotham, they realised that hardly any women's history had actually been written (and that which had was yet to be unearthed), so [they] decided to focus on the contemporary position of women instead.

As Graessle's sticker campaign showed, feminist organising was already under way—there had been the highly influential 1968 strike for equal pay by female machinists at Ford's Dagenham plant; and a 1969 women's issue of the revolutionary newspaper, *Black Dwarf*. But the activity was disparate, disconnected, and it was therefore unclear how many people would turn up at Ruskin. Rowbotham says that they were expecting "perhaps a hundred or two hundred people." Five hundred showed up. "Everybody arrived with their sleeping bags on Friday night," she says, "which was turmoil, and then they managed to extend the conference into the Oxford Union, an extraordinarily stiff environment that was meant to produce male orators who would become prime ministers. I remember being really scared of speaking in that room."

> 'As a child I had been very angry about being a girl, in terms of the way that I was treated, because the boys and the men had all the power.'

In *Once a Feminist*, Wandor writes that papers were given on "the family, motherhood, delinquency, women and the economy, the concept of 'women's work,' [and] equal pay," among others. Mary Kennedy, who was also at the conference, says that "there was a real buzz of excitement. As a child I had been very angry about being a girl, in terms of the way that I was treated, because the boys and the men had all the power. Then, here came this turning point, and we were all able to speak out."

The conference was organised by Alexander, with another young woman at Ruskin, Arielle Aberson, who would sadly die in a car accident a few months later. Alexander remembers the conference as exciting, and hugely hard work. There were many distinct leftwing groups in attendance, including Marxist-Leninists "who were most forthcoming to volunteer to take minutes," says Graessle, "then rewrote them to suit their view of history." There was also a small group who caused a dramatic confrontation when they painted slogans such as "Down with penis envy" over Ruskin and beyond. "Arielle and I had to negotiate between the police and them, between the student body and them, between the conference and them," says Alexander. "We got the brunt of it. They were a very small group, and they were very disruptive."

> 'It's hard to convey now the excitement of discovering what it meant to be a woman, and .. conceiving of it . . . [as a] collective and social issue.'

A Time of Excitement

Still, the general mood was unbridled optimism. Catherine Hall, who was involved with a women's group in Birmingham and had come to feminist consciousness after having her first child, describes it as a "utopian moment. . . . It's hard to convey now the excitement of discovering what it meant to be a woman, and to have a language to talk about that, and not conceiving of it as an individual issue, but a collective and social issue. That was what was most important. The recognition that we shared a feeling and experiences that had a name."

What followed was years of intense activity. Alexander came down to London after finishing at Ruskin that summer, and became involved with her local women's group, the women's liberation workshop office, and the night cleaners' campaign—"You name it," she says. Hall began a women's liberation playgroup, and Wandor compiled *The Body Politic*, a collection of feminist writing, including a number of papers from the conference.

"It was a time when you could be a 29-hour-a-day activist," says Wandor, partly because of economic conditions. "We could manage to live on fairly small amounts of money and be flexible," says Rowbotham, "and we all lived in shared houses."

There were many more conferences, building on the demands that had been made at the end of that first get-together. Ruskin had finished with a session called "Where are we going?" facilitated by Graessle, where all those in attendance voted unanimously on four demands: equal pay; equal education and opportunity; 24-hour nurseries; free contraception and abortion on demand. (The list of the movement's demands would swell over the years.)

Germaine Greer's *The Female Eunuch* and Kate Millett's *Sexual Politics* were both published in 1970, and there was a major demonstration at the Miss World contest that year, in which feminist activists flour-bombed the stage, in protest at women's objectification. (The reaction of the host, Bob Hope? "Pretty girls don't have these problems.") In 1971 there was the first National Women's Liberation Movement march—an event immortalised in Sue Crockford's film, *A Woman's Place*, in which groups of women sarcastically sing the ditty "Keep Young and Beautiful" as they stride forth. In 1975, the *Times* [of London] reported that there were "more than 1,500 groups of women around the country meeting fairly regularly"; that same year, the Equal Pay Act came into force. There was a huge amount of activism around rape and male violence—in 1979, for instance, the Southall Black Sisters began their work against domestic violence and legal injustice.

After the 1970s

But by the end of the decade, the tumult was dying down. It was partly exhaustion, says Alexander. It simply isn't possible to work at such a clip for ever. Then there were internal divisions—a chart produced in 1979 defined 13 distinct types of British feminist, including "eurocommunists", "humanists" and "redstockings." There was the fact that those who had been in their early to mid-20s in 1970 were now building careers and families, and so their personal circumstances were changing. And then there were the social conditions. When Margaret Thatcher became prime minister in 1979, the political tenor of the country shifted radically.

Feminism continued—the activism surrounding violence against women, for instance, has never died away—but that defining moment was gone. And in recent years, the outlook has been that young women aren't interested in the movement, that feminism is now, at best, slightly embarrassing—associated with flaming bras and battered dungarees—and at worst, completely dead. Which is a shame, since there's still so much to do. Just take that first women's liberation demand: equal pay. There has been improvement on this in the past four decades, but as Ceri Goddard, chief executive of the women's campaign group, the Fawcett Society, points out, women are still paid 16.4% less than men for full-time work. "And I think one of the reasons that the pay gap is still so stark," she says, "is to do with a lack of progress on some of the other tasks of the women's movement—particularly nurseries."

But in fact, in recent years, young women do seem to have been rising again. The women of the 1970 conference have noticed this. Rowbotham, Hall and Alexander all went on to become academics, and Rowbotham says that for a long time her students seemed uneasy about feminism, "but in the last two years, there seems to have been this reawakening of interest." . . .

For young feminists today, there's a sense of being part of a worldwide movement, which wasn't so true in 1970. As Zohra Moosa, women's rights adviser at Action-Aid, says, there are grassroots women's rights campaigns now across the globe: in Central and South America, "there's lots of work around political representation. In certain parts of Africa it's around leadership, and reforms to the law around violence against women. A huge amount of activity."

Four decades later, the movement seems revitalised, born anew, that sense of optimism suddenly recaptured. And it's not as if you have to look far to see the signs. Just this morning, on my way into work, I saw a sticker on a sexist poster. The slogan? "This ad degrades women."

A United Nations Treaty Forbids Discrimination Against Women

United Nations

From its inception, the United Nations has endorsed the principle of human rights for everyone in the world, including equal rights for men and women. However, this fundamental provision of its charter proved not to be enough to prevent discrimination against women, the following UN document says. In many countries they are not yet considered equal to men. The UN therefore developed a legally binding treaty to guarantee women's rights, which was adopted in 1979 and went into force in 1981 after twenty nations had ratified it. It gives women everywhere the right to vote and hold public office and aims to end discriminatory cultural attitudes toward women's role in society.

SOURCE. "Short History of CEDAW Convention" and "Introduction to Full Text of the Convention," UN Women, 2009. www.un.org/womenwatch. Copyright © 2009 by UN Women. All rights reserved. Reproduced by permission.

Equality of rights for women is a basic principle of the United Nations. The Preamble to the Charter of the United Nations sets as one of the Organization's central goals the reaffirmation of "faith in fundamental human rights, in the dignity and worth of the human person, in the equal rights of men and women". Article 1 proclaims that one of the purposes of the United Nations is to achieve international cooperation in promoting and encouraging respect for human rights and for fundamental freedoms for all without distinction as to, *inter alia* [among other things] sex. By the terms of the Charter, the first international instrument to refer specifically to human rights and to the equal rights of men and women, all members of the United Nations are legally bound to strive towards the full realization of all human rights and fundamental freedoms. The status of human rights, including the goal of equality between women and men, is thereby elevated: a matter of ethics becomes a contractual obligation of all Governments and of the UN.

The International Bill of Human Rights strengthens and extends this emphasis on the human rights of women. The Universal Declaration of Human Rights proclaims the entitlement of everyone to equality before the law and to the enjoyment of human rights and fundamental freedoms without distinction of any kind and proceeds to include sex among the grounds of such impermissible distinction. The International Covenant on Economic, Social and Cultural Rights and the International Covenant on Civil and Political Rights, both of 1966, which translate the principles of the Declaration into legally binding form, clearly state that the rights set forth are applicable to all persons without distinction of any kind and, again,

> The fact of women's humanity proved insufficient to guarantee them the enjoyment of their internationally agreed rights.

put forth sex as such a ground of impermissible distinction. In addition, each Covenant specifically binds acceding or ratifying States to undertake to ensure that women and men have equal right to the enjoyment of all the rights they establish.

The International Bill of Human Rights, combined with related human rights treaties, thus lays down a comprehensive set of rights to which all persons, including women, are entitled. However, the fact of women's humanity proved insufficient to guarantee them the enjoyment of their internationally agreed rights. Since its establishment, the Commission on the Status of Women (CSW) has sought to define and elaborate the general guarantees of non-discrimination in these instruments from a gender perspective. The work of CSW has resulted in a number of important declarations and conventions that protect and promote the human rights of women. . . .

Although these instruments reflected the growing sophistication of the UN system with regard to the protection and promotion of women's human rights, the approach they reflected was fragmentary, as they failed to deal with discrimination against women in a comprehensive way. In addition, there was concern that the general human rights regime was not, in fact, working as well as it might to protect and promote the rights of women. Thus, the General Assembly, on 5 December 1963, adopted its resolution 1921 (XVIII), in which it requested the Economic and Social Council to invite the CSW to prepare a draft declaration that would combine in a single instrument international standards articulating the equal rights of men and women. . . .

A Binding Treaty to End Discrimination Against Women

The 1960s saw the emergence, in many parts of the world, of a new consciousness of the patterns of discrimination against women and a rise in the number of organizations committed to combating the effect of such discrimination. The adverse impact of some development policies on women also became apparent. In 1972, five years after the adoption of the Declaration and four years after the introduction of a voluntary reporting system on the implementation of the Declaration by the Economic and Social Commission, the CSW considered the possibility of preparing a binding treaty that would give normative force to the provisions of the Declaration and decided to request the Secretary-General to call upon UN Member States to transmit their views on such a proposal. The following year, a working group was appointed to consider the elaboration of such a convention. In 1974, at its twenty-fifth session and in the light of the report of this working group, the Commission decided, in principle, to prepare a single, comprehensive and internationally binding instrument to eliminate discrimination against women. This instrument was to be prepared without prejudice to any future recommendations that might be made by the United Nations or its specialized agencies with respect to the preparation of legal instruments to eliminate discrimination in specific fields.

The text of the Convention on the Elimination of All Forms of Discrimination against Women was prepared by working groups within the Commission during 1976 and extensive deliberations by a working group of the Third Committee of the General Assembly from 1977 to 1979. Drafting work within the Commission was encouraged by the World Plan of Action for the Implementation of the Objectives of the International Women's Year, adopted by the World Conference of the International Women's Year held in Mexico City in 1975, which called for a convention

> The Convention entered into force—faster than any previous human rights convention.

on the elimination of discrimination against women, with effective procedures for its implementation. Work was also encouraged by the General Assembly which had urged the Commission on the Status of Women to finish its work by 1976, so that the Convention would be completed in time for the 1980 Copenhagen mid-decade review conference (World Conference on the United Nations Decade for Women: Equality, Development and Peace). Although suggestions were made to delay completion of the text for another year, the Convention on the Elimination of All Forms of Discrimination against Women was adopted by the General Assembly in 1979 by votes of 130 to none, with 10 abstentions. . . .

At the special ceremony that took place at the Copenhagen Conference on 17 July 1980, 64 States signed the Convention and two States submitted their instruments of ratification. On 3 September 1981, 30 days after the twentieth member State had ratified it, the Convention entered into force—faster than any previous human rights convention had done—thus bringing to a climax United Nations efforts to codify comprehensively international legal standards for women. . . .

Provisions of the Treaty

Among the international human rights treaties, the Convention takes an important place in bringing the female half of humanity into the focus of human rights concerns. The spirit of the Convention is rooted in the goals of the United Nations: to reaffirm faith in fundamental human rights, in the dignity and worth of the human person, in the equal rights of men and women. The present document spells out the meaning of equality and how it can be achieved. In so doing, the Convention establishes not only an international bill of rights for women, but also an agenda for action by countries to guarantee the enjoyment of those rights.

In its preamble, the Convention explicitly acknowledges that "extensive discrimination against women continues to exist", and emphasizes that such discrimination "violates the principles of equality of rights and respect for human dignity". As defined in article 1, discrimination is understood as "any distinction, exclusion or restriction made on the basis of sex . . . in the political, economic, social, cultural, civil or any other field". The Convention gives positive affirmation to the principle of equality by requiring States parties to take "all appropriate measures, including legislation, to ensure the full development and advancement of women, for the purpose of guaranteeing them the exercise and enjoyment of human rights and fundamental freedoms on a basis of equality with men" (article 3).

The agenda for equality is specified in fourteen subsequent articles. In its approach, the Convention covers three dimensions of the situation of women. Civil rights and the legal status of women are dealt with in great detail. In addition, and unlike other human rights treaties, the Convention is also concerned with the dimension of human reproduction as well as with the impact of cultural factors on gender relations.

The legal status of women receives the broadest attention. Concern over the basic rights of political participation has not diminished since the adoption of the Convention on the Political Rights of Women in 1952. Its provisions, therefore, are restated in article 7 of the present document, whereby women are guaranteed the rights to vote, to hold public office and to exercise public functions. This includes equal rights for women to represent their countries at the international level (article 8). The Convention on the Nationality of Married Women—adopted in 1957—is integrated under article 9 providing for the statehood of women, irrespective of their marital status. The Convention, thereby, draws attention to the fact that often women's legal status has been linked to marriage, making them dependent on their husband's nationality rather than individuals in their own right. Articles 10, 11 and 13, respectively, affirm women's rights to non-discrimination in education, employment and economic and social activities. These demands are given special emphasis with regard to the situation of rural women, whose particular struggles and vital economic contributions, as noted in article 14, warrant more attention in policy planning. Article 15 asserts the full equality of women in civil and business matters, demanding that all instruments directed at restricting women's legal capacity "shall be deemed null and void". Finally, in article 16, the Convention returns to the issue of marriage and family relations, asserting the equal rights and obligations of women and men with regard to choice of spouse, parenthood, personal rights and command over property.

Protection of Women's Reproductive Rights

Aside from civil rights issues, the Convention also devotes major attention to a most vital concern of women, namely their reproductive rights. The preamble sets the tone by stating that "the role of women in procreation should not be a basis for discrimination". The link between discrimination and women's reproductive role is a matter of recurrent concern in the Convention. For example, it advocates, in article 5, "a proper understanding of maternity as a social function", demanding fully shared responsibility for child-rearing by both sexes. Accordingly, provisions for maternity protection and childcare are proclaimed as essential rights and are incorporated into all areas of the Convention, whether dealing with employment, family law, health care or education. Society's obligation extends to offering social services, especially child-care facilities, that allow individuals to combine family responsibilities with work and participa-

tion in public life. Special measures for maternity protection are recommended and "shall not be considered discriminatory" (article 4). "The Convention also affirms women's right to reproductive choice. Notably, it is the only human rights treaty to mention family planning. States parties are obliged to include advice on family planning in the education process" (article 10.h) and to develop family codes that guarantee women's rights "to decide freely and responsibly on the number and spacing of their children and to have access to the information, education and means to enable them to exercise these rights" (article 16.e).

The third general thrust of the Convention aims at enlarging our understanding of the concept of human rights, as it gives formal recognition to the influence of culture and tradition on restricting women's enjoyment of their fundamental rights. These forces take shape in stereotypes, customs and norms which give rise to the

Japan's ambassador to Denmark (seated) signs the UN's Convention on the Elimination of All Forms of Discrimination against Women on July 17, 1980, at a special ceremony in Copenhagen. (AP Photo/EH.)

multitude of legal, political and economic constraints on the advancement of women. Noting this interrelationship, the preamble of the Convention stresses "that a change in the traditional role of men as well as the role of women in society and in the family is needed to achieve full equality of men and women". States parties are therefore obliged to work towards the modification of social and cultural patterns of individual conduct in order to eliminate "prejudices and customary and all other practices which are based on the idea of the inferiority or the superiority of either of the sexes or on stereotyped roles for men and women" (article 5). And Article 10.c mandates the revision of textbooks, school programmes and teaching methods with a view to eliminating stereotyped concepts in the field of education. Finally, cultural patterns which define the public realm as a man's world and the domestic sphere as women's domain are strongly targeted in all of the Convention's provisions that affirm the equal responsibilities of both sexes in family life and their equal rights with regard to education and employment. Altogether, the Convention provides a comprehensive framework for challenging the various forces that have created and sustained discrimination based upon sex.

> The Convention provides a comprehensive framework for challenging . . . discrimination based upon sex.

Some Women Were Not Happy with How Liberation Changed Their Lives

Susan Faludi

In the following viewpoint, an American journalist discusses the backlash against women's liberation. She observes that in the 1980s the media have been saying that the fight for equality has been won, that an Equal Rights Amendment is no longer needed, and that as a result women are more unhappy than they were before. According to the media, professional women are suffering from stress, single women complain about a shortage of men, and women without children are depressed. And yet, the author says, the majority of women believe that the women's movement did improve their lives and further effort should be made to achieve full equality. Susan Faludi is a Pulitzer Prize-winning journalist and the author of *Backlash:*

SOURCE. Susan Faludi, "Introduction: Blame It on Feminism," *Backlash: The Undeclared War Against American Women*. New York: Crown Publishing, 1991. Copyright © 1991 by Crown Publishing. All rights reserved. Reproduced by permission.

The Undeclared War Against American Women, from which this excerpt is taken, as well as several other books.

To be a woman in America at the close of the 20th century—what good fortune. That's what we keep hearing, anyway. The barricades have fallen, politicians assure us. Women have "made it," Madison Avenue cheers. Women's fight for equality has "largely been won," *Time* magazine announces. Enroll at any university, join any law firm, apply for credit at any bank. Women have so many opportunities now, corporate leaders say, that we don't really need equal opportunity policies. Women are so equal now, lawmakers say, that we no longer need an Equal Rights Amendment. Women have "so much," former President Ronald Reagan says, that the White House no longer needs to appoint them to higher office. Even American Express ads are saluting a woman's freedom to charge it. At last, women have received their full citizenship papers.

And yet. . . .

Behind this celebration of the American woman's victory, behind the news, cheerfully and endlessly repeated, that the struggle for women's rights is won, another message flashes. You may be free and equal now, it says to women, but you have never been more miserable.

This bulletin of despair is posted everywhere—at the newsstand, on the TV set, at the movies, in advertisements and doctors' offices and academic journals. Professional women are suffering "burnout" and succumbing to an "infertility epidemic." Single women are grieving from a "man shortage." The *New York Times* reports: Childless women are "depressed and confused" and their ranks are swelling. *Newsweek* says: Unwed women are "hysterical" and crumbling under a "profound crisis of confidence." The health advice manuals inform: High-powered career women are stricken with unprecedented outbreaks of "stress-induced disorders," hair loss, bad nerves, alcoholism, and even heart attacks. The psychology books advise: Independent women's loneliness represents "a major mental health problem today." Even founding feminist Betty Friedan has been spreading the word: she warns that women now suffer from a new identity crisis and "new 'problems that have no name.'"

How can American women be in so much trouble at the same time that they are supposed to be so blessed? If the status of women has never been higher, why is their emotional state so low? If women got what they asked for, what could possibly be the matter now?

Backlash Against Women's Liberation

The prevailing wisdom of the past decade [the 1980s] has supported one, and only one, answer to this riddle: it must be all that equality that's causing all that pain. Women are unhappy precisely because they are free. Women are enslaved by their own liberation. They have grabbed at the gold ring of independence, only to miss the one ring that really matters. They have gained control of their fertility, only to destroy it. They have pursued their own professional dreams—and lost out on the greatest female adventure. The women's movement, as we are told time and again, has proved women's own worst enemy.

"In dispensing its spoils, women's liberation has given my generation high incomes, our own cigarette, the option of single parenthood, rape crisis centers, personal lines of credit, free love, and female gynecologists," Mona Charen, a young law student, writes in the *National Review*, in an article titled "The Feminist Mistake." "In return it has effectively robbed us of one thing upon which the happiness of most women rests—men." The *National Review* is a conservative publication, but such charges against the women's movement are not confined to its pages. "Our generation was the human sacrifice" to the women's movement, *Los Angeles Times* feature writer Elizabeth Mehren contends in a *Time* cover story. Baby-boom women like her, she says, have been duped by feminism: "We believed the rhetoric." In *Newsweek*, writer Kay Ebeling dubs feminism "The Great Experiment That Failed" and asserts "women in my generation, its perpetrators, are the casualties." Even the beauty magazines are saying it: *Harper's Bazaar* accuses the women's movement of having "lost us [women] ground instead of gaining it."

> [The media] hold the campaign for women's equality responsible for nearly every woe besetting women, from mental depression to meager savings accounts.

In the last decade, publications from the *New York Times* to *Vanity Fair* to the *Nation* have issued a steady stream of indictments against the women's movement, with such headlines as "when feminism failed" or "the awful truth about women's lib." They hold the campaign for women's equality responsible for nearly every woe besetting women, from mental depression to meager savings accounts, from teenage suicides to eating disorders to bad complexions. The "Today" show says women's liberation is to blame for bag ladies. A guest columnist in the *Baltimore Sun* even proposes that feminists produced the rise in slasher movies. By making the "violence" of abortion more acceptable, the author reasons, women's rights activists made it all right to show graphic murders on screen.

At the same time, other outlets of popular culture have been forging the same connection: in Hollywood films, of which *Fatal Attraction* is only the most famous, emancipated women with condominiums of their own slink wild-eyed between bare walls, paying for their liberty with an empty bed, a barren womb. . . .

Popular psychology manuals peddle the same diagnosis for contemporary female distress. "Feminism, having promised her a stronger sense of her own identity, has given her little more than an identity crisis," the best-selling advice manual *Being a Woman* asserts. The authors of the era's self-help classic *Smart Women/Foolish Choices* proclaim that women's distress was "an unfortunate consequence of feminism," because "it created a myth among women that the apex of self-realization could be achieved only through autonomy, independence, and career." . . .

Some academics have signed on to the consensus, too—and they are the "experts" who have enjoyed the highest profiles on the media circuit. On network news and talk shows, they have advised millions of women that feminism has condemned them to "a lesser life." Legal scholars have railed against "the equality trap." Sociologists have claimed that "feminist-inspired" legislative reforms have stripped women of special "protections." Economists have argued that well-paid working women have created "a less stable American family." And demographers, with greatest fanfare, have legitimated the prevailing wisdom with so-called neutral data on sex ratios and fertility

Glenn Close (center) and Michael Douglas (right) both won awards for their 1987 film *Fatal Attraction*. Some writers have drawn parallels between the women's liberation movement and the increase in violent and psychotic female characters like the one played in that movie by Close. (AP Photo/Bob Galbraith.)

trends; they say they actually have the numbers to prove that equality doesn't mix with marriage and motherhood.

Some Women Feel "Liberation" Was a Mistake

Finally, some "liberated" women themselves have joined the lamentations. In confessional accounts, works that invariably receive a hearty greeting from the publishing industry, "recovering Superwomen" tell all. In *The Cost of Loving: Women and the New Fear of Intimacy*, Megan Marshall, a Harvard-pedigreed writer, asserts that the feminist "Myth of Independence" has turned her generation into unloved and unhappy fast-trackers, "dehumanized" by careers and "uncertain of their gender identity." Other diaries of mad Superwomen charge that "the hardcore feminist viewpoint," as one of them puts it, has relegated educated executive achievers to solitary nights of frozen dinners and closet drinking.

> The word may be that women have been "liberated," but women themselves seem to feel otherwise.

The triumph of equality, they report, has merely given women hives, stomach cramps, eye-twitching disorders, even comas.

But what "equality" are all these authorities talking about? . . .

The word may be that women have been "liberated," but women themselves seem to feel otherwise. Repeatedly in national surveys, majorities of women say they are still far from equality. . . .

The afflictions ascribed to feminism are all myths. From "the man shortage" to "the infertility epidemic" to "female burnout" to "toxic day care," these so-called female crises have had their origins not in the actual conditions of women's lives but rather in a closed system that starts and ends in the media, popular culture, and

The Conflict Between Feminists and Homemakers

Feminism implicitly degrades home-makers by calling for women to seek fulfillment outside the home, which discredits those women who are fulfilled by being wives and mothers. Feminism explicitly belittles home-makers by labeling their work as drudgery, as mundane, as ungrati-fying, and as glorified babysitting. Feminism's call for women to go beyond the housewife role, to step into the male world of paid labor, denies the importance and the satis-faction derived by those content with their homemaker status.

As one local pro-family activ-ist explains: "The feminists want all women to work. But all women don't want to work. I talk to women all the time around here who really want to stay home with their children. It's not because they're misled or not liber-ated. They honestly want to stay home with their children. I've seen women who have to work [extremely] torn up by having to leave their nine-month-old babies."

Or, in another pro-family activist's words: "The women's liberation move-ment looks down on the housewife. She should be the most respected person as she is bringing up future generations. But women's liberation puts her down and says, 'All she does is stay home all day and wash dirty diapers.' ERA won't do anything for these women."

In this way, the conflict between feminists and homemakers is a tug-of-war between two lifestyles. There is no peaceful coexistence between those women following traditional ways and those women seeking new paths, new careers. Rather than the lifestyle of each being accepted and valued, social conservatives view feminists as promoting new roles for women at the expense of the old, thereby devaluing the homemaker's status.

SOURCE. Rebecca Klatch, Women of the New Right, *Temple University Press, 1988. [As posted at www.h-net. org/~hst203/readings/klatch.html.]*

advertising—an endless feedback loop that perpetuates and exaggerates its own false images of womanhood.

Women themselves don't single out the women's movement as the source of their misery. To the contrary, in national surveys 75 to 95 percent of women credit the feminist campaign with improving their lives, and a similar proportion say that the women's movement should keep pushing for change. Less than 8 percent think the women's movement might have actually made their lot worse.

CHAPTER 3

Personal Narratives

An Activist Tells Why She Supports the Women's Liberation Movement

Phyllis LaFata, interviewed by Ann B. Lever

In the following interview, a founding member of the St. Louis, Missouri, chapter of the National Organization for Women (NOW) explains that she felt guilty because she didn't like housework or raising children, and that when her husband left her, she thought she was a failure. Then she got involved in volunteer work that led to a job, went back to college to get a master's degree, and became active in the women's movement. Eventually she became the movement's spokesperson to the media in her city. She says, at the time of the interview in 1972, that while changing laws concerning women was helpful, it was also important to change the attitudes instilled in children at home and in school. Phyllis LaFata was director of public relations for the Young Women's Christian

SOURCE. Phyllis LaFata, "Interview with Ms. Phyllis Lafata," *Women in the Seventies Project*, February 15, 1972. Copyright © State Historical Society of Missouri—St. Louis Research Center. All rights reserved. Reproduced by permission.

Association (YWCA) in St. Louis. Ann B. Lever is a retired litigator formerly with Legal Services of Eastern Missouri.

*A*nn B. Lever: *When would you say that you had any consciousness about women's problems, women's rights, a women's movement?*

Phyllis Lafata: I wish I could say that I was early on, but I really wasn't. As I told them this morning, when I read Betty Friedan's *Feminine Mystique*, I knew that I was one of those women who didn't like doing housework, who didn't like raising children, who didn't like staying at home, and yet, I thought that made me strange, you know? And I felt very guilty about this. I'm supposed to like these things. I'm supposed to want to do them, and there's something wrong with me that I don't, and it's a tremendous relief to know that you're really not strange, you know. There are a lot of other women who feel like you do and it's not strange and there's no reason to feel guilty about it. But not feeling guilty came much later, not at that particular point and time, just a realization that I wasn't a weirdo. I was just one among many, of course that's how the National Organization for Women originated. Women decided to get together do something about changing ideas about women.

Were there any sorts of experiences that maybe changed your consciousness? Anything else that happened to you that you read? Any people you met?

Well I had known people that I met. I did volunteer work for the Young Women's Christian Association [YWCA], which is a fantastic organization because it's made up entirely of women. Even the entire staff is women, which is unusual. . . . The volunteers are all women. So there's no real put down. When you come in as a volunteer, you don't get relegated to washing the dishes. Your ideas are important, and your feelings are important and they have value, and there's no male domination or competition. That was very instrumental in my development. You know coming from somebody who was hurting and injured and incapable of functioning, because I did reach that point and time where I became a vegetable. You know, I didn't like what I had, I didn't know how to change it. I didn't know what to do about it, and so I just regressed. I slept away my life. I got up and did what I had to do and I went to bed. . . . But I did get in doing volunteer work for this women's organization, people listened when I talked. I do have something to say, I am not stupid. My husband had never been supportive because his own ego was a little frail, plus the fact that he was from an old Italian family where the man is the strong father figure who believed that women should be barefoot in the winter and pregnant in the summer. Anything I did was threatening to him, and so I never could manage to fit the role that he thought I should fit. I couldn't fight back. I couldn't communicate to him with any kind of feedback, and so that was how it went.

> In doing volunteer work for this women's organization, people listened when I talked. I do have something to say.

When did you start working again?

I started working again when my husband left home. He just, like, walked out. While I had wanted a divorce for several years, [my mother said] "there are the children; there's been no divorce in your family. This isn't what you do," and then your own fears that you keep putting up. The nicest thing that he did for me besides give me the four children was to make the decision for me, because

I might never have been able to make that decision, [about] like you know, how to keep buying the groceries, how to keep paying the rent, when you haven't worked for sixteen years, what do you say when you go to look for a job, and where do you look? . . . If my husband had rejected me, then I was good for nothing, you know. Nobody could love me, nobody could like me. I couldn't do anything right, and you generalize that for your whole life situation. I am incompetent in every area. I am a loss. I am a total failure, and that's very hard to deal with. . . .

Becoming Independent

When did you go back to get your master's degree?

Well, I just kind of fell into this job at the "Y," you know, particularly the first one, and I knew it wasn't going to last, and I knew that agency did not pay particularly well, and knowing that I was getting practically no money from my husband, and I had a house and kids to raise, I thought, "I got to do something." And I wanted to get a degree in psychology. I thought I could be a psychologist, and then I talked to people who, well, I couldn't afford Washington University [in St. Louis] and the University of Missouri-St. Louis didn't have that program. . . . So I compromised . . . and went into guidance and counseling. And I thought that was some kind of a goal to set. Now I could say, "I did that, all by myself, I did that." I find as life goes on, there's nothing so exhilarating or so exciting or so satisfying as being completely independent. . . .

> As life goes on, there's nothing so exhilarating or so exciting or so satisfying as being completely independent.

It is. I agree with you. What about your current involvement in the women's movement? What organizations are you involved with?

I have a very interesting association and very interesting history in the women's movement. I got all fired up before the National Organization for Women [NOW] established a chapter in St. Louis. We got a group of women together and we were going to start our own thing, and while we were hassling around exactly how we were going to do it, because the YWCA is involved in the women's movement not as deeply as I would like to see it particularly at the local level, but somewhat involved. Before we really got through the organizational stages, we heard about the National Organization for Women, that there were some women who were going to establish a chapter in St. Louis. I was one of the founding members and have been a member ever since. That was, golly, about two years ago; it was a few months before the first national strike on August 26. I got deeply involved in that and have been ever since. On National Strike Day, we started from thc YWCA, we invaded the men's bar on the [riverboat] Becky Thatcher, which is now no longer a men's bar I'm glad to report. There was a great deal of radio and television coverage, and somehow I got to be the spokesman for women's liberation in the city of St. Louis. . . .

Really how the whole thing evolved has just amazed me. I sat in on the first meeting of the women's political caucus. There was a small group of us who got together at that first original organizational meeting. I have not done as much work as I'd like to in that group. I hope to be able to do more. But I act as kind of a—they feed information to me and I give it out to other women, someone who calls and says "I have this problem," and I say, "Well, where you really ought to be is working on the laws or working on this or working on that." And so I direct them to where they want to go. I managed to get the [St. Louis] Post-Dispatch want ads desegregated, single-handedly, me and a friendly attorney. I work in just all kinds of areas. I also do counseling for the clergymen consultation service one night a week. I run a group counseling thing for divorced women. So I work around in all kinds of different areas.

Have you personally been in a cell group or in a consciousness raising group?

I have sat in on [one]; there is only one group per se that I know is going on now, and we've tried to start some others. I've been in on some that were very disappointing and very bad. Even supposedly liberated women. I sat in on one and I really could have vomited, because they sat and talked about typical women things, but the sad thing was they got off on divorce and that's one reason why I started a group for divorced women per se. They were projecting all the hostility against the man, and there's no divorce that does not involve two people. I am not this all because of him. It was all anger and hate. And the woman is never going to make an adjustment to herself and to her life with that kind of feeling. You have to accept responsibility for yourself and you have to learn to know what problems are yours as a person rather than because you had a bad marriage or because of your husband. . . .

You were talking about before NOW came to St. Louis, that you were together with some other women thinking about sort of forming some sort of organization. How did you get together with them? What had happened to you that made you want to organize?

Well, we had been talking and reading. We read *The Feminine Mystique*, other things about the women's movement, and the more we got together—these were mostly women who worked for the "Y"—the more we got together and the more we talked about the sea of discrimination and injustices and needs, and then there was just the supportiveness of getting together and talking over those things, which is really what a conscience-level raising is. And I've seen fantastic things done in a conscience-level raising group. I talked about a bad one. I've seen a good one. I've seen a woman whose males in her family told her she was so poorly coordinated she would never learn to drive an automobile. She accepted this, it's what men say, that's what her son said, that's what her husband said, and so she was housebound and isolated for lack of transportation. But the women in the group said, "Of course, you can, of course you're coordinated, of course you're intelligent, of course you can learn to drive." And she learned to drive an automobile. . . .

> I would really like to see. . . people being able to develop their potentials . . . without any kind of regard to sex or race or religion.

Hope for Future Changes

If you had a vision of what the good society ought to look like in terms of women, what would it look like? . . .

In terms of women? Well, you can't frame it all in terms of women, you have to frame it in terms of people. There are a lot of things that we haven't discussed, like the black woman and her relationship to the movement, and her relationship to the world, and the importance of well, for instance, welfare [which] they say is one of the biggest problems in the United States today. There is no way we can begin to eliminate welfare until women get equal pay for equal work and equal opportunity, because the major members of the family below the poverty level are women, and the major portion of those are black women, and it's increasing rather than decreasing. The number of poverty level families headed by black men is decreasing, not rapidly, but it is showing an appreciable amount, and with black women it's going up. Black women are not really into the movement, because they got this whole structure of the black family which I'm sure you don't want to go into and discuss because that would take another hour. What we really want to see, and what I would really like to see, and it's a pat phrase, but people being able to develop their potentials, their abilities, their talents, whatever they are without any kind of regard to sex or race or religion or any of those good things, just to become whatever they have the capability of being without any outside discrimination. The family will change. The structure of the family, I even think, will change.

> Technologically we're on the moon, but when it comes to people, we're still back in the Stone Age.

What do you think is responsible for what's wrong [with] women's lives, about sex discrimination? What lies behind it? How in sort of a larger sense do you change it? Do you change the economic structure or is it some sort of psychological—

Well, it's all those things and we'll be able to change. We can change the laws, and by changing the laws we will change the economic thing. We will remove, hopefully, some discrimination, attitudes is another whole bag. Technologically we're on the moon, but when it comes to people, we're still back in the Stone Age. Our Constitution is based on the English Common Law which regarded women as chattel, belongings. They belonged to their husband, they had no rights separate from their husband, and we have no rights today. Without the Equal Rights Amendment, women have no rights in the Constitution except the right to vote. There's one state in the Union where a married woman's clothing is still owned by her husband.

Do you think the NOW approach of changing laws, of changing state ways will really change attitudes?

Well, we're working in other areas. For instance, we work in task forces and we have one in education. . . . Because from the time a baby is born, is when it all begins. Little boy babies are given toy tractors to duel over, and little girls are given rag dolls to clasp to their breast. And the boy baby is thrown up into the air, jostled around, and the girl baby is tenderly cradled and cooed over. . . . And then you get into school, and girls for toys get nurses kits, and boys get doctors kits. Girls, you ask them, they're going to grow up to be a mommie, and how many kids are they going to have . . . the whole bit. Your textbooks discriminate against all kinds of women. Mother is always in the backyard or in the kitchen, father is always doing something meaningful, comes home from work. It never rains, nobody's ever sick, nobody's ever poor, nobody's ever divorced in a child's book in school. There are no single parent families. Can you imagine how kids from broken families feel? . . .

So it really starts way back there. . . . Liberated women, or the ones who follow us, are going to have to raise their children differently and demand. We were talking about education, we have gone to where we are examining textbooks, and we're finding cases of discrimination, and we're going to confront the publishers and the school systems and say, "look, fellows, this is what you are doing to our children."

A Young Woman Tells Why She Stopped Opposing Women's Liberation

Joan

The following viewpoint is an excerpt from the memoir of a woman who initially felt that women's liberation was not important. She explains that she changed her mind when she realized she had, like others around her, accepted inequality between men and women. She also realized that it was foolish of her to put up an act and pretend she had the personality people thought women should have. Instead, she says, she longed for the opportunity to grow and to change society. This article first appeared in *Womankind*, the newspaper of the Chicago Women's Liberation Union.

I remember when I first thought about whether Women's Liberation was relevant to me. I decided against it. My good (male) friend had gently hinted that this Women's Liberation thing was attracting quite a few of the "cool" girls at school and maybe I should look into it. I thought it over, then explained that I didn't share those women's problems. After all, I wasn't too shy to talk in my classes. I talked as much as the men. Anyway, I had always said that I liked feeling inferior to a man. I was looking for (and having trouble finding) a man who was stronger than me, smarter than me, and in general just a touch better than me at everything—someone I could look up to and lean on.

When I heard that part of the Women's Liberation line was about how women should be permitted to be as loud and aggressive as they wanted, I was a bit more turned on. Not that I considered myself an aggressive bitch type. On the contrary, I had worked long and hard to be able to be aggressive AND still feminine. I knew that if I wanted to talk as much as I did and say the things that I did, I had damn well be charming at the same time. I wasn't into eyelash-batting but there were ways that I walked, sat, dressed, etc. that "saved" me from being labeled a castrating bitch. Then I read the *BITCH Manifesto*, by and about a woman [Jo Freeman, under her pseudonym Joreen] who wanted to be her normal aggressive self without trying to be charming too, and it really affected me. I could feel how that woman felt (like I was trying to avoid feeling) and I could see how a woman like me was being accepted precisely because I wasn't as "bad" as her.

I realized the whole thing was ridiculous—women being told to play this absurd game of having a certain kind of personality and actually going along with it. Why should I have to do a song and dance routine to be accepted for what I really am? I felt like a fool. Instead of my usual feelings of jealousy of other women, I felt angry that I was feeling jealous. I had been manipulated into that feeling, so we would all keep trying for the stupid image. It was the contest approach. We were all in the Miss America pageant. How humiliating.

Recognizing Injustice

Seeing how unequal things were between men and women, and how women (me too) had accepted it, helped me to see how unequal things were for many people in our society. And the whole society just accepts it, even though some people are starving and others are millionaires. In my own middle-class life, I sometimes feel like I'm starving, when I'm sitting home with my two kids while my husband is out doing his exciting work-of-his-own-choice. I starve for novelty, stimulation, the opportunity to grow and help others grow and change things. It's unfair that my life should be determined by my sex, and it makes me furious—too angry to put up with it much longer. That people are actually starving for food is so much worse that it seems unbearable.

Recognizing the unfairness of the situation is liberating in itself. I like not having to worry about clothes anymore, and I don't mind being scorned by people who would have me be a stupid object. It's a pleasure to have warm, wonderful feelings for other women—not just to see them as friends rather than enemies, but to consider how we women can mean so much to each other as not to need men. Struggling with Women's Liberation is also very difficult, especially since I am trying to work out a happy relationship with a man, something I hope but don't know is a possibility. Since I have become a part of the Women's Liberation Movement, I am more and more convinced that our Movement is right. Unlike so much else that I and my sisters have become involved in; I haven't and won't lose interest, and I'll never turn back.

> " It's unfair that my life should be determined by my sex, and it makes me furious—too angry to put up with it much longer. "

An Author of Novels About Women's Liberation Recalls Her Involvement

Alix Kates Shulman, interviewed by Charlotte Templin

In the following interview, a woman recounts that she became a writer because she wanted to reach an audience that needed to hear about the women's liberation movement, which at the time was just beginning. She explains that she believes fiction can convey the feel of an era in a way that nonfiction cannot. Her novels were successful because readers responded emotionally to them and started to think about things they hadn't thought of before. Though the women's movement accomplished a great deal, she says, there is still a lot to be done to achieve equality between men and women. Alix Kates Shulman is the author of twelve books, including *Memoirs of an Ex-Prom Queen* and other

SOURCE. Alix Kates Shulman, interviewed by Charlotte Templin, "An Interview with Alix Kates Shulman," *Missouri Review*, Winter 2001. Copyright © 2001 by the Missouri Review. All rights reserved. Reproduced by permission.

novels about women's liberation. Charlotte Templin is a writer and editor of books about feminism and teaches at the University of Indianapolis.

Charlotte Templin: When did you make the decision to be a writer?

Alix Kates Shulman: I did not intend to be a writer. I first wanted to be a lawyer, like my father. Then I got bit by the bug of philosophy and wanted to be a philosophy professor. I went to graduate school and quickly discovered it was impossible for a woman in those days—this was the early fifties—to be a philosopher, so I gave that up. I didn't know what I was going to do, but then when I became a feminist, when the movement started in the late sixties, I started writing because I had something urgent to say. My first novel, *Memoirs of an Ex-Prom Queen*, is the product of that urgency. I knew that there was another view of women's experience that hadn't been expressed in fiction, or hardly ever, a view that was just beginning to take hold in this country. I wanted to dramatize it. And I knew that there was an audience who needed to hear it. I wasn't sure if I could reach them, or whether I could do it well. But I knew we had to come together somehow. That was why I became a writer. . . .

You are not only a novelist who chronicled the women's movement but you have had a role in the movement from its earliest days. How did you get your first information about the women's movement?

From the radio, actually. Some women announced their meeting on the air, and I went with my friend. It was a very early women's liberation group, one of several small, nameless spinoffs of the large New York Radical Women. Immediately I thought, "This is important. This is going to give an explanation for the various aspects of my misery that will enable me to change it." I understood for the first time that things did not have to be the way they were, that they could be changed. A lot of us felt that way, and that's how the movement started. It was a thrilling thing to be alive and to be there at that moment. It changed my life.

> The movement for women's liberation was . . . a feeling all over the country that things must be different.

You said in A Good Enough Daughter *that when you were a young adult the want ads were separated into male and female positions. It is hard for my students to imagine a world like that.*

You couldn't apply for any job listed for men. I know it's hard to believe now.

Burning Questions *commemorates the early days of the women's movement. How did your impulses to create fiction and to preserve history go together?*

Usually, ordinary histories don't get the emotional feel of a period. That's what a novel can do. The movement for women's liberation was about an emotional transformation, an explosion, a feeling all over the country that things must be different, and ideas about how they should be. I think fiction can capture that kind of thing better than other genres because in fiction you can explore the feelings of your characters—the before and the after. Maybe a scholar could do that in biography, but then the feelings would just be one person's. Fiction is ideally suited to re-creating the important emotional aspects of history. One important part of historical recording is to get people of another generation to understand the feelings, the passion that went into social transformation. That's why oral history is so valuable. . . .

Historical Accuracy

Is the part of Burning Questions *that deals with the FBI historical?*

The FBI was infiltrating the women's movement all along. *The World Split Open*, by Ruth Rosen, has a whole chapter about the CIA and the FBI, the infiltration and the spies. There was a big FBI file on the movement that the feminists got hold of through the Freedom of Information Act. The FBI file of Zane, the character in *Burning Questions*, is sort of based on mine.

> Everybody who was involved in any kind of sixties left movement had an FBI file.

You had an FBI file?

Oh, yeah. Everybody who was involved in any kind of sixties left movement had an FBI file. I certainly did. It consisted mostly of reviews of my books. I mean, they hadn't a clue.

The history of the movement that you portray in the novel is very accurate. For example, you describe the demonstrations at the Miss America Pageant. There were demonstrations inside and outside. Alice Echols mentions in Daring to Be Bad *that you bought the tickets for those who went inside.*

Yes, I did. I was married, and my husband and I had a joint checking account. But I didn't earn any money; he earned all of the money. I had earned money before I had children, but then I left my job. This was prefeminism, pre-women's movement, and things were very different. I didn't feel I had permission to use money from our joint checking account for anything that my husband didn't approve of—certainly not something subversive like women's liberation—so buying those tickets was one of my first great gestures of independence.

Did you go inside?

I was outside. We marched around, and we shouted our slogans, and we threw all these accoutrements of "women's oppression," like high-heeled shoes, *Playboy* magazines, brooms, girdles and curlers, into a freedom trash can. There were many different actions on the boardwalk. Interestingly, the inspiration for *Memoirs of an Ex-Prom Queen* came to me on the boardwalk. I suddenly could see my life in terms of our junior high and high school beauty focus. I was never a prom queen myself, but I knew that milieu very well. . . .

Was the novel [Burning Questions] also about self-discovery?

It's about self-discovery in the sense that women's liberation drew for its power on the self-discovery of each of its participants. You could call it collective self-discovery. That has to be part of Zane's story because that is the story of women's liberation.

The Response from Readers

What kind of response did the novel get from the other feminist pioneers?

Feminists were all very, very supportive of it. The novel was trashed by the *New York Times* by a notorious anti-feminist. One of the very first projects of a group called the Feminist Writers' Guild was to protest the treatment of *Burning Questions* by the *Times*, which gave the review a full page and said, "This novel will set back the cause of women fifty years."

Many reviewers were baffled by women's liberation at the time. They often said that feminist novelists were harming the cause of women. Here's a review of Prom Queen *from the* Christian Science Monitor, *for example, that criticizes Sasha's attitudes and choices and notes that the first wave of suffragettes seems to have been forgotten.*

Yes, don't we wish that suffragettes had been remembered? Things might have been different for Sasha's generation. It's clear that those reviewers didn't know what we were talking about. When I first wrote *Prom Queen,* I thought the only people who would get it (because I meant it to be funny) would be the ten women in my women's group. I was writing it for them. And then a lot of people got it.

> There is still nothing like equality in jobs, in family. There's just an awareness that inequality is not acceptable.

It sold very well.

The way it got to be a big seller was that it was handed around in the publishing houses before it was in paperback. All of the secretaries, as they were called then—now they would be editorial assistants—said, "Look at this." The publishing houses were largely run by men, and they didn't have any idea why all the "girls" were so excited about my book, but they knew the book had an appeal, so at the paperback auction they all bid on it. . . .

Do you know any sales figures?

Not for *Burning Questions.* I know that *Prom Queen* sold over one million copies in paperback. Maybe thirty-five thousand in hardcover. And people passed it around. It had a lot of readers. People often say to me now, "Your work changed my life." I'm sure that's an exaggeration, but they say it had a big effect on them and enabled them to change. I'm not sure I believe that a book will cause someone to change. It was the movement that did that, but maybe the book put them in contact with the movement. Or maybe the book made them think about things they hadn't before, and then there was a movement there for those ready for it. . . .

The Current State of the Movement

What is the state of the women's movement right now [2001]?

I think that everything remains to be done. Not that we haven't accomplished a great deal; we certainly have. But we need to go further. There is still nothing like equality in jobs, in family. There's just an awareness that inequality is not acceptable, and that's good. In the early seventies, it was considered perfectly proper that the want ads should be segregated "Help wanted: men/Help wanted: women," and that men should get three times as much money as women. That isn't any longer considered acceptable, but pay is still not anywhere near equal. There is a lot of gender segregation. You still have many poor women who work in women-only jobs. In the family, in most cases, only women have the double job of working outside the home and taking care of the family. Of course, sexual violence is still rampant. And abortion rights, without which there can be no equality, are always

Beauty standards in the fashion industry are cited by some as evidence of the continuing oppression of women. On average, models weigh ten pounds less than they did a decade ago. **(AP Photo/Stuart Ramson.)**

being chipped away. I don't think there's any area of our lives where we can say, "Okay, let's move on. Everything's fine. Let's look for another area." In the last decade or so, the greatest advances have been made internationally. In some ways, I think the situation here is worse now. The gap between rich and poor has widened since the sixties, and the greatest number of poor people are women and children. The beauty standards are so much more stringent than they were twenty or thirty years ago. Models are on average ten pounds slimmer than they were a decade ago. Bulimia and anorexia are going on in junior high school. In the advertising industry, the sexual exploitation of female images is worse than it was. Not that I'm in favor of any kind of censorship. I'm only in favor of people becoming more and more aware, so they will demand change.

A Black Feminist Recalls the Publication of Her First Book

Michele Wallace

In the following memoir excerpt, a black author tells the story behind the writing and publication of her first book, *Black Macho and the Myth of the Superwoman*, which dealt with black men's sexist attitudes toward women. It brought her a great deal of media attention and praise from feminists, but she was attacked by many African Americans who disagreed with her views. Michele Wallace is a black feminist and the author of many books. She is a professor of English at the City University of New York.

In 1979, when I was 26 years old and veering wildly between thinking I knew it all and I knew nothing, I wrote a book that went off like a bomb. In *Black Macho and the Myth of the Superwoman*, I indiscreetly

SOURCE. Michele Wallace, "Memoirs of a Premature Bomb-thrower," *The Village Voice*, February 13, 1996. Copyright © 1996 by Village Voice Media. All rights reserved. Reproduced by permission.

blurted out that sexism and misogyny were a near-epidemic in the black community and that black feminism had the cure. I went from obscurity to celebrity to notoriety overnight. Quite suddenly, I was a guest on the *Today Show*, the *Phil Donahue Show*, and the six o'clock news from Newark to Pomona; I was reviewed, attacked, and debated in *Essence*, the *Nation*, the *New York Times*, the *Washington Post*, the *Village Voice* and the *Black Scholar*. The harshest and most hurtful words came from my own people, even my mother. Too young to know better and too old to shut up, I had written the book from hell. Of course, it didn't really come from hell. Like all the explosive writing going on in those days, it came from life.

Being a feminist in the '70s had a lot to do with the times; for me, it also had everything to do with being the daughter of the ambitious, fiercely militant, and driven black female artist Faith Ringgold. My family specialized in superwomen of various sorts and women who just couldn't cope on almost any level.

From an early age, you were expected to declare which you would be. I always thought Faith and I came to feminism at the same time, but I now suspect that I was following her lead in the way that a child sometimes can without being aware of it, especially since I was an inveterate mama's girl right through my early twenties. In the early '70s, I often assisted my mother on her various radical forays into the antiwar, anti-imperialist art movement of the times. With Faith's help, I started Women Students and Artists for Black Art Liberation. . . .

When I finally graduated from CCNY [City College of New York] in 1974, it seemed like a liberation of sorts. I considered myself a veteran feminist by this time. For reasons that now escape me, I had adopted a pseudo-African guise, wearing the headwrap called a gele, long dresses, sandals, no makeup, and so forth. I was sometimes mistaken for a Muslim, which won me

some respect on the street, more than you might get in a miniskirt. Yet here I was, this very opinionated black feminist who had real problems with the Black Muslim agenda. . . .

Around this time Faith and I helped found the National Black Feminist Organization, along with a whole bunch of the usual suspects. . . . About a year later the sisterhood would begin meeting at [author] Alice Walker's house in Brooklyn to talk about what, if anything, black women writers should do or say about feminism.

An Ambition to Write

Somewhere along the line I had become incredibly ambitious as a writer. (With a mother like Faith, there weren't too many other choices.) I had started doing sexy short pieces for *Ms.*, and in 1974 Ross Wetzasteon invited me to write for the [*Village*] *Voice*. He took me to Karen Durbin, who edited my first *Voice* essays—one called "Anger in Isolation: A Black Feminist's Search for Sisterhood" and the other about growing up a black American princess in the Harlem of the '50s and '60s. It was with these articles that my identity as a black feminist began to get seriously public. . . .

The *Voice* articles brought me my book editor, Joyce Johnson . . . at Dial Press, which also published most of James Baldwin's work. Margo [Jefferson] introduced me to Maxine Groffsky, who became my literary agent. In 1975, Maxine helped me draft a proposal for a book on black women, and Joyce got me a modest advance ($12,500), whereupon I immediately quit my *Newsweek* job and moved away from home uptown with Mom to a mouse-ridden apartment on Greene Street.

Within a few months I had whipped up the core of what I thought would be a single chapter on black men. But Joyce argued that it should be the centerpiece of the book and that I needed only another large section on black women. We then began the laborious two-year

Photo on previous page: Faith Ringgold poses in front of one of her paintings in 1999. In the 1970s, she and her daughter Michele Wallace started the Women Students and Artists for Black Art Liberation. **(Anthony Barboza/Getty Images.)**

process of editing "Black Macho" and constructing the much more difficult section of the book that would be called "The Myth of the Superwoman."

Since my money was low, my guardian angel Margo recommended me to Helen Epstein for a job teaching journalism at NYU [New York University]. At 24, I was suddenly a university professor (actually my rank was lecturer) in a school with almost no black faculty. After I moved into NYU housing in Washington Square Village, it was a common occurrence to be frantically queried by middle-aged white women in fur coats as to whether or not I had any free days for housework. I was always so stunned I can't recall what I would say. I wasn't used to living around white folks. . . .

> 'There is a profound distrust, if not hatred . . . between black men and black women that has been nursed along largely by white racism.'

As we approached the galley stage, Robin Morgan submitted my text for review to [feminist and editor of *Ms.*] Gloria Steinem and Alice Walker. Needless to say, they liked it a lot (which isn't to say they wouldn't later change their minds), and through the ministrations of Susan McHenry, a new black editor, I ended up with a double excerpt and my face on the cover of *Ms.*

Becoming a Celebrity

Then the whirlwind began: over the way I looked and dressed for public appearances, the way I spoke, what I did and didn't say. While Dial Press wondered whether I should be described as a black feminist in their press materials, *Ms.* wondered whether I was up to snuff as a black feminist spokesperson (I was not). . . .

Then the sniper attacks started rolling in. But what could I expect after allowing Dial to feature the most inflammatory paragraph in the book on the jacket cover? "I am saying . . . there is a profound distrust, if not hatred," my inner child proclaimed in black type against a white background, "between black men and black women that has been nursed along largely by white racism but also by an almost deliberate ignorance on the part of blacks about the sexual politics of their experience in this country."

When I did readings and talks, black folks came at me with book in hand, quoting chapter and verse. I was completely at a loss to explain how the book had actually come about. In a way, I still am. I think now that *Black Macho and the Myth of the Superwoman* was one of those manuscripts that was never supposed to see print. The result of an unhappy alliance between a perfectionist aesthete and a young, nihilistic, black-feminist militant, half-crazed, and sexually frustrated maniac, the text could only hope to crash and burn, and this it promptly did.

Did I have doubts, then and later, about *Black Macho*? Sure. About its grace and wisdom, certainly, although not about its essential, upsetting truth. But I never stopped believing that it is better to blurt truth even in a headlong way than it is to keep silent for the sake of peace. That's what much of women's liberation was about: breaking our patient, fear silence. *Black Macho* documents a crucial stage in my development, and perhaps in yours, in learning the lesson that we're all human and that perfectibility is a crock, that men are people too, and that there aren't any really good answers in life, just questions. When Verso asked if they could reprint the book six years ago, I readily agreed. *Black Macho* belongs, warts and all, with other documents of the heady times of the '60s and '70s.

> I never stopped believing that it is better to blurt truth even in a headlong way than it is to keep silent for the sake of peace.

CHRONOLOGY

1920   Women win the right to vote through the Nineteenth Amendment to the US Constitution.

1923   The Equal Rights Amendment (ERA), authored by Alice Paul, who led the campaign for women's suffrage (the right to vote), is introduced in the US Congress for the first time. It is introduced in every session of Congress thereafter.

1963   Betty Friedan's best seller *The Feminine Mystique* is published, launching what is now known as the Second Wave women's movement (the First Wave was the fight for suffrage).

1964   Title VII of the Civil Rights Act bars employment discrimination by private employers, employment agencies, and unions based on sex, among other grounds.

1966   The National Organization for Women (NOW) is established.

The term "women's liberation" first appears in print.

1968   A group of radical feminists protests the Miss America Pageant in Atlantic City, New Jersey, and gains national media attention for the liberation movement.

The Equal Employment Opportunity Commission (EEOC) bans sex-segregated help wanted ads in newspapers, a ruling upheld in 1973 by the Supreme Court.

Shirley Chisholm becomes the first black woman elected to the US House of Representatives.

1970   NOW organizes the Women's Strike for Equality on the fiftieth anniversary of the ratification of the Nineteenth Amendment. Fifty thousand women march on Fifth Avenue in New York, with marches also occurring in fifty other cities.

1971   For the first time, the US Supreme Court, in *Reed v. Reed*, strikes down a law that treated men and women differently.

The ERA is approved by the House of Representatives.

1972   On March 22, the ERA is approved by the Senate and submitted to the states for ratification. Twenty-two of the required thirty-eight states ratify it in the same year.

Phyllis Schlafly forms the National Committee to Stop ERA, starting a campaign by conservative women to defeat ratification of the amendment.

Congress passes Title IX of the 1972 Educational Amendments to the Civil Rights Act to enforce sex equality in education, forcing educational institutions to support women's sports.

Shirley Chisholm runs for the Democratic Party's nomination for US president, becoming the first woman and first African American to seek the presidency.

1973   Eight more states ratify the ERA. Only five other states do so between 1974 and 1977, and none after.

In *Roe v. Wade*, the Supreme Court establishes a woman's right to have an abortion.

1975   The United Nations sponsors the First International Conference on Women in Mexico City.

1977   The First National Women's Conference is held in Houston, Texas, attended by twenty thousand women from every US state.

1978   In July, a hundred thousand people march in Washington, D.C., to demand an extension of the ERA ratification deadline. The House and Senate vote to extend it until 1982. Five states rescind their ratification of the ERA between 1973 and 1979.

1979   The Pregnancy Discrimination Act bans employment discrimination against pregnant women, stating a woman cannot be fired, placed on leave, or denied a job or a promotion because she is or may become pregnant.

1981   Sandra Day O'Connor becomes the first woman appointed to the US Supreme Court.

1982   The ERA falls three states short of ratification when the deadline expires. Supporters continue to reintroduce it in every session of Congress.

FOR FURTHER READING

Books

Mary Frances Berry, *Politics, Women's Rights, and the Amending Process of the Constitution*. Bloomington: Indiana University Press, 1988.

Susan Brownmiller, *In Our Time: Memoir of a Revolution*. New York: Dial, 1999.

Dorothy Sue Cobble, *The Other Women's Movement: Workplace Justice and Social Rights in Modern America*. Princeton: Princeton University Press, 2004.

Gail Collins, *When Everything Changed: The Amazing Journey of American Women from 1960 to the Present*. New York: Little, Brown, 2009.

Stephanie Coontz, *A Strange Stirring: The Feminine Mystique and American Women at the Dawn of the 1960s*. New York: Basic Books, 2011.

Donald T. Critchlow, *Phyllis Schlafly and Grassroots Conservatism: A Woman's Crusade*. Princeton: Princeton University Press, 2005.

Rachel DuPlessis and Anne Snitow, eds., *The Feminist Memoir Project*. New York: Three Rivers Press, 1998.

Sara M. Evans, *Personal Politics: The Roots of Women's Liberation in the Civil Rights Movement and the New Left*. New York: Knopf, 1979.

Sara M. Evans, *Tidal Wave: How Women Changed America at Century's End*. New York: Free Press, 2003.

Susan Faludi, *Backlash: The Undeclared War Against American Women*. New York: Crown, 1991.

Betty Friedan, *The Feminine Mystique*. New York: Norton, 1963.

Betty Friedan, *The Second Stage*. New York: Summit Books, 1986.

Carol Giardina, *Freedom for Women: Forging the Women's Liberation Movement, 1953–1970*. Gainesville: University of Florida Press, 2010.

Sylvia Ann Hewlett, *A Lesser Life: The Myth of Women's Liberation in America*. New York: Morrow, 1986.

Alice Kessler-Harris, *In Pursuit of Equity: Women, Men, and the Quest for Economic Citizenship in 20th-Century America*. New York: Oxford University Press, 2001.

Jane J. Mansbridge, *Why We Lost the ERA*. Chicago: University of Chicago Press, 1986.

Donald G. Mathews and Jane Sherron De Hart, *Sex, Gender, and the Politics of ERA: A State and the Nation*. New York: Oxford University Press, 1990.

Linda Nicholson, ed., *The Second Wave: A Reader in Feminist Theory*. New York: Routledge, 1997.

Ruth Rosen, *The World Split Open: How the Modern Women's Movement Changed America*. New York: Viking, 2000.

Phyllis Schlafly, *Feminist Fantasies*. Dallas: Spence Publishing, 2003.

Deborah Siegel, *Sisterhood, Interrupted: From Radical Women to Grrls Gone Wild*. New York: Macmillan, 2007.

Gloria Steinem, *Outrageous Acts and Everyday Rebellions*. New York: Holt, 1995.

Gilbert Y. Steiner, *Constitutional Inequality: The Political Fortunes of the Equal Rights Amendment*. Washington, DC: Brookings Institute, 1985.

Anne M. Valk, *Radical Sisters: Second-Wave Feminism and Black Liberation in Washington, D.C.* Urbana: University of Illinois Press, 2010.

Periodicals

Jessica Bennett, Jesse Ellison, and Sarah Ball, "Are We There Yet?" *Newsweek*, March 19, 2010.

Leslie Bennetts, "Women Stage Fifth Ave. Rally For Rights Amendment," *New York Times*, July 1, 1981.

Martha Brant, Eve Conant, and Jennie Yabroff, "From Barricades to Blogs," *Newsweek*, October 22, 2007.

Andree Brooks, "NOW Seeks to Rekindle Enthusiasm of Past," *New York Times*, December 1, 1985.

Dana Caneday, "Advocates of Equal Rights Amendment Resume Their Fight," *New York Times*, May 3, 2003.

Mona Charen, "The Feminist Mistake," *National Review*, March 23, 1984.

Adam Clymer, "Time Runs Out For Proposed Rights Amendment," *New York Times*, July 1, 1982.

George Dullea, "Women Give Up Careers to Crusade for Equality," *New York Times*, November 8, 1981.

Sam J. Ervin Jr., "E.R.A.'s Time Is Gone," *New York Times*, August 1, 1983.

Allison Kasic, "Forty Years of Feminism: Nag, Nag, Nag," *Weekly Standard*, August 7, 2006.

Elizabeth Kolbert, "Firebrand," *New Yorker*, November 7, 2005.

Kristen Luker, "Losers in a Zero-Sum Game., *New York Times Book Review*, October 19, 1986.

David John Marley, "Phyllis Schlafly's Battle Against the ERA and Women in the Military," *Minerva: Quarterly Report on Women and the Military*, Summer, 2000.

Louis Menand, "Books as Bombs: Why the Women's Movement Needed 'The Feminine Mystique,'" *New Yorker*, January 24, 2011.

Nancy Munger and Laura Roskos, "Human Rights for Women," *Peace and Freedom*, Fall 2009.

Kate O'Beirne, "Bread & Circuses," *National Review*, October 13, 1997.

Kate O'Beirne, "Founding Mother," *National Review*, November 7, 2005.

Jane Perlez, "NOW's Funds Soar Suggesting Extent of Women's Power," *New York Times*, May 20, 1982.

Jane Perlez, "Ratification Defeat Leaves Rights Law on Uneven Path," *New York Times*, June 27, 1982.

Sean Price, "Housewives 1, Feminists 0: Divided Over Women's Rights, The Two Sides Waged a Battle Over the Equal Rights Amendment," *New York Times Upfront*, March 11, 2002.

Francine Prose, "Giant Steps for Womankind, but Still Miles to Go," *New York Times*, October 20, 2009.

Phyllis Schlafly, "Left Schemes to Revive ERA," *Human Events*, April 16, 2007.

Winston Williams, "Thousands March for Equal Rights," *New York Times*, June 7, 1982.

Alan Wolfe, "Mrs. America," *New Republic*, October 3, 2005.

Websites

Duke University Special Collections Library (http://scriptorium.lib.duke.edu/wlm). A large collection of articles about women's liberation from the 1960s and 1970s.

Eagle Forum (www.eagleforum.org/ERA). The political organization founded by Phyllis Schlafly, who led the opposition to the Equal Rights Amendment. Its section on the ERA includes information about the STOP ERA campaign as well as more recent material strongly opposing the amendment's revival.

The Equal Rights Amendment (www.equalrightsamendment .org). A project of the Alice Paul Foundation, a not-for-profit corporation aiming to enhance public awareness of the life and work of Alice Paul, who was the original author of the Equal Rights Amendment. It offers detailed information about the background of the amendment and its political history in the US Congress and in the states.

National Organization for Women (www.now.org). The largest organization of feminist activists in the United States, with the goal of taking action to bring about equality for all women. Its site contains extensive material on current political and social issues as well as the ERA.

National Women's History Project (www.nwhp.org). A clearinghouse providing information and training in multicultural women's history for educators, community organizations, parents, and students wanting to expand their understanding of women contributions to US history. Its site contains a detailed history of the women's rights movement.

Sophia Smith Collection (www.smith.edu/library/libs/ssc). The women's history archive at Smith College, an internationally recognized repository of manuscripts, archives, photographs, periodicals, and other primary sources in women's history. The site contains a number of online exhibits plus the Voices of Feminism Oral History Project, which includes transcripts and some videos.

INDEX